PRENTICE HALL FOUNDATIONS OF PHILOSOPHY SERIES

| | |
|---|---|
| *Virgil Aldrich* | Philosophy of Art |
| *William Alston* | Philosophy of Language |
| *David Braybrooke* | Philosophy of Social Science |
| *Roderick M. Chisholm* | Theory of Knowledge, 3E |
| *William Dray* | Philosophy of History |
| *Joel Feinberg* | Social Philosophy |
| *Frederick Ferré* | Philosophy of Technology |
| *William K. Frankena* | Ethics, 2E |
| *Martin P. Golding* | Philosophy of Law |
| *Carl Hempel* | Philosophy of Natural Science |
| *John H. Hick* | Philosophy of Religion, 4E |
| *Gerald C. MacCallum* | Political Philosophy |
| *D. L. C. Maclachlan* | Philosophy of Perception |
| *Wesley C. Salmon* | Logic, 3E |
| *Jerome Shaffer* | Philosophy of Mind |
| *Richard Taylor* | Metaphysics, 3E |

*Elizabeth Beardsley and Tom Beauchamp, Editors*

*Monroe Beardsley, Founding Editor*

Fourth Edition

# PHILOSOPHY OF RELIGION

## John H. Hick

Claremont Graduate School
Claremont, California

PRENTICE HALL, *Englewood Cliffs, New Jersey* 07632

Library of Congress Cataloging-in-Publication Data

Hick, John.
    Philosophy of religion / John Hick. -- 4th ed.
        p.    cm. -- (Prentice-Hall foundations of philosophy series)
    Includes bibliographical references.
    ISBN 0-13-662628-9
    1. Religion--Philosophy.    I. Title.    II. Series.
BL51.H494    1990
    200'.1--dc20                                        89-36841
                                                           CIP

Editorial/production supervision: *Alison D. Gnerre*
Manufacturing buyer: *Carol Bystrom/Mike Woerner*

 © 1990, 1983, 1973, 1963 by Prentice-Hall, Inc.
A Division of Simon & Schuster
Englewood Cliffs, New Jersey 07632

Printed in the United States of America

10  9  8  7  6  5  4  3  2  1

ISBN 0-13-662628-9

Prentice-Hall International (UK) Limited, *London*
Prentice-Hall of Australia Pty. Limited, *Sydney*
Prentice-Hall Canada Inc., *Toronto*
Prentice-Hall Hispanoamericana, S.A., *Mexico*
Prentice-Hall of India Private Limited, *New Delhi*
Prentice-Hall of Japan, Inc., *Tokyo*
Simon & Schuster Asia Pte. Ltd., *Singapore*
Editora Prentice-Hall do Brasil, Ltda., *Rio de Janeiro*

# Contents

# Foundations of Philosophy

Many of the problems of philosophy are of such broad relevance to human concerns, and so complex in their ramifications, that they are, in one form or another, perennially present. Though in the course of time they yield in part to philosophical inquiry, they may need to be rethought by each age in the light of its broader scientific knowledge and deepened ethical and religious experience. Better solutions are found by more refined and rigorous methods. Thus, one who approaches the study of philosophy in the hope of understanding the best of what it affords will look for both fundamental issues and contemporary achievements.

Written by a group of distinguished philosophers, the Foundations of Philosophy Series aims to exhibit some of the main problems in the various fields of philosophy as they stand at the present stage of philosophical history.

While certain fields are likely to be represented in most introductory courses in philosophy, college classes differ widely in emphasis, in method of instruction, and in rate of progress. Every instructor needs freedom to change his course as his own philosophical interests, the size and makeup of his class, and the needs of his students vary from year to year. The volumes in the Foundations of Philosophy Series—each complete in itself, but complementing the others—offer a new flexibility to the instructor, who can create his own textbook by combining several volumes as he wishes, and choose different combinations at different times. Those volumes that are not used in an introductory course will be found valuable, along with other texts or collections of readings, for the more specialized upper-level courses.

*Elizabeth Beardsley / Monroe Beardsley / Tom L. Beauchamp*

# Preface

This book, addressed primarily to students in philosophy and religion departments, was first published in 1963. Revised editions, reflecting the continuous development of the subject, were published in 1973 and 1983. The appearance of this fourth edition after a shorter gap than the ten years separating the earlier editions is due to the accelerated pace of change in the subject. Indeed, the philosophy of religion is one of the most active areas of philosophical research today. This fourth edition includes a new chapter (Chapter 6) on contemporary work in the epistemology of religion, as well as a general updating of the other chapters. To make room for the fresh material, without adding to the size and expense of the volume, several sections of other chapters have been dropped.

I hope that this little book may continue to introduce students, in the seven languages in which it is available, to this fascinating and immensely important subject.

John Hick
Claremont Graduate School,
Claremont, California 91711

# Introduction

---

## WHAT IS THE PHILOSOPHY OF RELIGION?

What is the philosophy of religion? It was at one time generally understood to mean religious philosophizing in the sense of the philosophical defense of religious convictions. It was seen as continuing the work of "natural," distinguished from "revealed," theology.[1] Its program was to demonstrate rationally the existence of God, thus preparing the way for the claims of revelation. But it seems better to call this endeavor "natural theology" and to term the wider philosophical defense of religious beliefs "apologetics." Then we may reserve the name "philosophy of religion" for what (by analogy with philosophy of science, philosophy of art, etc.) is its proper meaning, namely, *philosophical thinking about religion*.

Philosophy of religion, then, is not an organ of religious teaching. Indeed, it need not be undertaken from a religious standpoint at all. The atheist, the agnostic, and the person of faith all can and do philosophize about religion. Philosophy of religion is, accordingly, not a branch of theology (meaning by "theology" the systematic formulation of religious beliefs), but a branch of philosophy. It studies the concepts and belief systems of the religions as well as the prior phenomena of religious experience and the activities of worship and meditation on which these belief systems rest and out of which they have arisen.

Philosophy of religion is thus a second-order activity, standing apart from

[1]These terms are defined on pp. 57–58.

its subject matter. It is not itself a part of the religious realm but is related to it as, for example, the philosophy of law is related to the realm of legal phenomena and to juridical concepts and modes of reasoning, or the philosophy of art to artistic phenomena and to the categories and methods of aesthetic discussion. The philosophy of religion is thus related to the particular religions and theologies of the world as the philosophy of science relates to the special sciences. It seeks to analyze concepts such as God, dharma, Brahman, salvation, worship, creation, sacrifice, nirvana, eternal life, etc., and to determine the nature of religious utterances in comparison with those of everyday life, scientific discovery, morality, and the imaginative expressions of the arts.

What, however, is religion? Many different definitions have been proposed. Some of these are phenomenological, trying to state that which is common to all the acknowledged forms of religion; for example, religion is "human recognition of a superhuman controlling power and especially of a personal God or gods entitled to obedience and worship" (*Concise Oxford Dictionary*). Others are interpretative. Thus there are psychological definitions—for example, "the feelings, acts, and experiences of individual men in their solitude, so far as they apprehend themselves to stand in relation to whatever they may consider the divine" (William James). Others are sociological—for example, "a set of beliefs, practices, and institutions which men have evolved in various societies" (Talcott Parsons). Others, again, are naturalistic—for example, "a body of scruples which impede the free exercise of our faculties" (Salomon Reinach) or, more sympathetically, "ethics heightened, enkindled, lit up by feeling" (Matthew Arnold). Yet others are religious definitions of religion—for example, "Religion is the recognition that all things are manifestations of a Power which transcends our knowledge" (Herbert Spencer), or again, "humanity's response to the divine."

But such definitions are all stipulative: they decide how the term is to be used and impose this in the form of a definition. Perhaps a more realistic view is that the word "religion" does not have a single correct meaning but that the many different phenomena subsumed under it are related in the way that the philosopher Ludwig Wittgenstein has characterized as family resemblance. His own example was the word "game." You cannot define a game as being played for pleasure (for some are played for profit), or as being competitive (for some are solo performances), or as requiring skill (for some depend on chance), or indeed it would seem by any single feature. Yet all these different kinds of game overlap in character with some other kinds, which in turn overlap in different ways with yet other kinds, so that the whole ramifying collection hangs together in a complex network of similarities and differences which Wittgenstein likened to the resemblances and differences appearing within a family.[2] We may apply Wittgenstein's idea to the word "religion."

[2]*Philosophical Investigations*, 2nd. ed., trans. G.E.M. Anscombe (Oxford: Basic Blackwell & Mott, Ltd., 1958), pp. 66–67.

Perhaps there is no one characteristic of everything that can be called a religion but rather a set of "family resemblances." In much religion there is the worship of a God or gods; but in Theravada Buddhism, for example, there is not. Again, religion often makes for social cohesion; yet in some strands it is aptly characterized as "what man does with his solitariness" (A. N. Whitehead). Again, religion often makes for the inner harmony of the individual; yet some of the greatest religious innovators seemed to their contemporaries to be unbalanced and even insane. The family resemblances model allows for such differences. It also allows us to acknowledge the similarities as well as the differences between more standard examples of religion and such secular faiths as Marxism. Marxism has its eschatological ideal of the ultimate class-less society, its doctrine of predestination through historical necessity, its scriptures, prophets, saints, and martyrs. Thus we can see it as sharing some of the features of the family of religions while lacking other and probably more central ones. But whether a movement is religious is not an all-or-nothing matter but a question of degree within a widely spreading network of resemblances and differences.

Within this ramifying set of family resemblances there is, however, one feature which is extremely widespread even though not universal. This is a concern with what is variously called salvation or liberation. This is probably not a feature of "primitive" or "archaic" religion, which is more concerned with keeping things on an even keel, avoiding catastrophe. However, all the great developed world faiths have a soteriological (from the Greek *soteria*, salvation) structure. They offer a transition from a radically unsatisfactory state to a limitlessly better one. They each speak in their different ways of the wrong or distorted or deluded character of our present human existence in its ordinary, unchanged condition. It is a "fallen" life, lived in alienation from God; or it is caught in the world-illusion of *maya*; or it is pervaded throughout by *dukkha*, radical unsatisfactoriness. They also proclaim, as the basis for their gospel, that the Ultimate, the Real, the Divine, with which our present existence is out of joint, is good, or gracious, or otherwise to be sought and responded to; the ultimately real is also the ultimately valuable. Completing the soteriological structure, they each offer their own way to the Ultimate—through faith in response to divine grace; or through total self-giving to God; or through the spiritual discipline and maturing which leads to enlightenment and liberation. In each case, salvation or liberation consists of a new and limitlessly better quality of existence which comes about in the transition from self-centeredness to Reality-centeredness.

In this discussion I have been following the conventional view of religions as clearly demarcated entities—Christianity, Hinduism, Buddhism, and so on. In fact, however, the picture is more complex than this, and in Chapter 9 I shall describe the important critique of the idea of "a religion" offered in our time by Wilfred Cantwell Smith.

In the meantime the discussion will focus upon the Judaic-Christian concept of God, which lies behind our western Atlantic civilization and still constitutes the main religious option within our culture. It will also be important to see how contemporary philosophical methods can be applied to the ideas of quite different religious traditions, and this will be done, as a sample, in relation to the Indian belief in reincarnation (Chapter 11). It is also necessary, in the "one world" of today, to face the problem of the apparently conflicting truth claims of the various religions. This issue, which constitutes one of the main growing points of the philosophy of religion today, will be explored in Chapter 9.

# CHAPTER 1

# The Judaic-Christian Concept of God

## MONOTHEISM

The terms used for the main ways of thinking about God are formed around either the Greek word for God, *theos*, or its Latin equivalent, *deus*.

Beginning at the negative end of the scale, *atheism* (not-God-ism) is the belief that there is no God of any kind; *agnosticism*, which means literally "not-know-ism," is in this context the belief that we do not have sufficient reason either to affirm or to deny God's existence. *Skepticism* simply means doubting. *Naturalism* is the theory that every aspect of human experience, including the moral and religious life, can be adequately described and accounted for in terms of our existence as gregarious and intelligent animals whose life is organic to our natural environment.

Moving to the positive side of the scale, *deism* can refer either to the idea of an "absentee" god who long ago set the universe in motion and has thereafter left it alone or, as an historical term, to the position of the eighteenth-century English deists, who taught that natural theology[1] alone is religiously sufficient. *Theism* (often used as a synonym for monotheism) is belief in a personal deity. *Polytheism* (many-gods-ism) is the belief, common among ancient peoples and reaching its classic expression in the west in ancient Greece and Rome, that there are a multitude of personal gods, each

[1]For a definition of *natural theology*, see pp. 57–58.

ruling a different department of life.[2] A person whose religion is a form of *henotheism* believes that there are many gods but restricts allegiance to one of them, generally the god of one's own tribe or people. *Pantheism* (God-is-all-ism) is the belief, perhaps most impressively expounded by some of the poets, that God is identical with nature or with the world as a whole. *Panentheism* (everything-in-God-ism) is the view that all things exist ultimately "in God." *Monotheism* (one-God-ism) is the belief that there is but one supreme Being, who is personal and moral and who seeks a total and unqualified response from human creatures. This idea first came to fully effective human consciousness in the words, "Hear, O Israel: The Lord our God is one Lord; and you shall love the Lord your God with all your heart, and with all your soul, and with all your might."[3] As these historic words indicate, the Semitic understanding of God, continued in Christianity and Islam, is emphatically monotheistic.

The Hebrew scriptures (which also constitute the "Old Testament" in the Christian Bible) document the rise of monotheism in constant but never fully resolved struggle with polytheism and henotheism. The God of the Hebrews was originally worshiped as a tribal god, Jahweh of Israel, over against such foreign deities as Dagon of the Philistines and Chemosh of the Moabites. But the insistent, though at first incredible, message of the great prophets of the eighth, seventh, and sixth centuries before the Christian era (above all, Amos, Hosea, first Isaiah, Jeremiah, and second Isaiah) was that Jahweh was not only the God of the Hebrews but the Maker of heaven and earth and the Judge of all history and of all peoples. The Hebrew prophets taught that although God had indeed summoned their own nation to a special mission as the living medium of his revelation to the world, he was not only their God but also Lord of the gentiles or foreigners. A great biblical scholar said, "Hebrew monotheism arose through the intuitive perception that a God who is righteous first and last must be as universal as righteousness itself."[4] The service of such a God must involve a responsibility not only to fellow members of the same "household of faith" but to all one's fellow creatures of every race and group.

It is a corollary of the prophets' teaching concerning the lordship of God over all life that there is no special religious sphere set apart from the secular

[2]For example, in the Greek pantheon, Poseidon (god of the sea), Ares (god of war), and Aphrodite (goddess of love).

[3]Deut. 6:4–5. Earlier than this, in the fourteenth century B.C.E., the Egyptian pharaoh Ikhnaton had established the sole worship of the sun god Aton but immediately after Ikhnaton's death this early monotheism was overcome by the prevailing national polytheism. NOTE: All biblical quotations, except where otherwise noted, are reprinted by permission and are taken from the Revised Standard Version of the Holy Bible (New York: Thomas Nelson & Sons). Copyright 1946, 1952 by the Division of Christian Education of the National Council of Churches.

[4]C. H. Dodd, *The Authority of the Bible*, 1929 (New York: Harper & Row, Publishers, Torchbooks, 1958), p. 111.

world but that the whole sweep of human existence stands in relation to God. Thus religion is secularized, or—to put it another way—ordinary life takes on a religious meaning. In the words of H. Richard Niebuhr:

The counterpart of this secularization, however, is the sanctification of all things. Now every day is the day that the Lord has made; every nation is a holy people called by him into existence in its place and time and to his glory; every person is sacred, made in his image and likeness; every living thing, on earth, in the heavens, and in the waters is his creation and points in its existence toward him; the whole earth is filled with his glory; the infinity of space is his temple where all creation is summoned to silence before him.[5]

The difficulty involved in maintaining such a faith in practice, even within a culture that has been permeated for centuries by monotheistic teaching, is evidenced by the polytheistic and henotheistic elements in our own life. A religiously sensitive visitor from another planet would doubtless report that we divide our energies in the service of many deities—the god of money, of a business corporation, of success, and of power, the status gods, and (for a brief period once a week) the God of Judaic-Christian faith. When we rise above this practical polytheism, it is generally into a henotheistic devotion to the nation, or to the American way of life, in order to enjoy our solidarity with an in-group against the out-groups. In this combination of elements there is no continuity with the pure monotheism of the prophets and of the New Testament, with its vivid awareness of God as the Lord of history whose gracious purpose embracing all life renders needless the frantic struggle to amass wealth, power, and prestige at the expense of others.

## INFINITE, SELF-EXISTENT

Judaic-Christian monotheism, finding its primary expressions in the commands and prayers, psalms and prophecies, parables and teachings of the Bible, has been philosophically elaborated and defined through the long history of Christian thought; and because Christianity has become a more theologically articulated religion than Judaism, most of our material will be taken from this source.

A basic idea which recurs is that God is infinite or unlimited.

It is this insistence that God is unlimited being that led Paul Tillich to hold that we should not say even that God *exists*, since this would be a limiting statement. "Thus the question of the existence of God can be neither asked nor answered. If asked, it is a question about that which by its very nature is above existence, and therefore the answer—whether negative or affirma-

[5]H. Richard Niebuhr, *Radical Monotheism and Western Culture* (New York: Harper & Row, Publishers, 1960), pp. 52–53.

tive—implicitly denies the nature of God. It is as atheistic to affirm the existence of God as it is to deny it. God is being-itself, not *a* being."[6] This paradox, as it must sound in the mouth of a theologian, that "God does not exist" is however not as startling as it may at first appear. It operates as a vivid repudiation of every form of belief in a finite deity. Tillich means, not that the term "God" does not refer to any reality, but that the reality to which it refers is not merely one among others, not even the first or the highest, but rather the very source and ground of all being. Tillich was, in effect, urging a restriction of the term "exists" to the finite and created realm, thereby rendering it improper either to affirm or to deny the existence of the infinite creator. But it is only on the basis of this restricted usage that Tillich repudiated the statement that God exists. He was emphasizing the point, which was familiar to the medieval scholastics, that the creator and the created cannot be said to exist in precisely the same sense.

God, then, according to Judaism and Christianity, is or has unlimited being, and the various divine "attributes" or characteristics are so many ways in which the infinite divine reality *is*, or exists, or has being.

First among these attributes we may place what the scholastics called *aseity* (from the Latin *a se esse*, being from oneself), usually translated as "self-existence." The concept of self-existence, as it occurs in the work of the great theologians, contains two elements:

1. God is not dependent either for existence or for characteristics upon any other reality. God has not been created by any higher being. There is nothing capable either of constituting or of destroying God. God just *is*, in infinite richness and plenitude of being as the ultimate, unconditioned, all-conditioning reality. In abstract terms, God has absolute ontological independence.

2. It follows from this that God is eternal, without beginning or end. If God had a beginning, there would have to be a prior reality to bring God into being; and in order for God's existence to be terminated, there would have to be some reality capable of effecting this. Each of these ideas is excluded by God's absolute ontological independence.

The divine eternity means more, however, than simply that God exists without beginning or end, as is indicated in this passage from Anselm (1033–1109):

Indeed You exist neither yesterday nor today nor tomorrow but are absolutely outside all time. For yesterday and today and tomorrow are completely in time; however, You, though nothing can be without You, are nevertheless not in place or time but all things are in You. For nothing contains You, but You contain all things.[7]

[6]Paul Tillich, *Systematic Theology* I (Chicago: University of Chicago Press and Welwyn, Hertfordshire: James Nisbet & Company Ltd., 1951), p. 237. Copyright 1951 by the University of Chicago.

[7]*Proslogion,* Chap. 19, trans. M. J. Charlesworth, *St. Anselm's Proslogion* (Oxford: Clarendon Press, 1965), pp. 141–43.

# CREATOR

God is conceived in the Judaic-Christian tradition as the infinite, self-existent Creator of everything else that exists. In this doctrine, creation means far more than fashioning new forms from an already given material (as a builder makes a house, or a sculptor a statue); it means creation out of nothing—*creatio ex nihilo*—the summoning of a universe into existence when otherwise there was only God. There are two important corollaries of this idea.

First, it entails an absolute distinction between God and the creation, such that it is logically impossible for a creature to become the Creator. That which has been created will forever remain the created. To all eternity the Creator is Creator and the creature is creature. Any thought of human beings becoming God is thus ruled out as meaningless by this conception of creation.

A second corollary is that the created realm is absolutely dependent upon God as its Maker and as the source of its continued existence. Hence we find that this radical notion of creation *ex nihilo* expresses itself in prayer and liturgy as a sense of dependence upon God from moment to moment. We have a part in the universe, not by some natural right, but by the grace of God, and each day is a gift to be received in thankfulness and responsibility toward the divine Giver.

What are the scientific implications of this idea? Does it entail that the creation of the physical universe took place at some specific moment in the far distant past?

Thomas Aquinas (1224/5–1274) held that the idea of creation does not necessarily rule out the possibility that the created universe may be eternal. It is, he thought, conceivable that God has been creative from all eternity, so that although the universe has a created and dependent status, it nevertheless did not have a beginning. He also held, however, that although the concept of creation does not in itself imply a beginning, Christian revelation asserts a beginning; and on this ground he rejected the idea of an eternal creation.[8] A different and perhaps more fruitful approach is suggested by Augustine's thought that the creation did not take place *in* time but that time is itself an aspect of the created world.[9] If this is true it may also be, as relativity theory suggests, that space-time is internally infinite—that is to say, from within the space-time continuum the universe is found to be unbounded both spatially and temporally. It may nevertheless, although internally infinite, depend for its existence and its nature upon the will of a transcendent Creator. This is the essence of the religious doctrine of creation: namely, that the universe as a spatiotemporal whole exists in virtue of its relation to God. Such a doctrine is

[8]*Summa Theologica*, Part I, Question 46, Art. 2. There is a good discussion of Aquinas's doctrine of creation in F. C. Copleston, *Aquinas* (Harmondsworth, Middlesex: Penguin Books Ltd., 1955), pp. 136f.

[9]*Confessions*, Book 11, Chap. 13; *City of God*, Book 11, Chap. 6.

neutral as between the various rival theories of the origin of the present state of the universe developed in scientific cosmology.[10]

Needless to say, the magnificent creation story in the first two chapters of the Book of Genesis is not regarded as a piece of scientific description by responsible religious thinkers today. It is seen rather as the classic mythological expression of the faith that the whole natural order is a divine creation. Indeed, this way of reading religious myths is very ancient, as the following passage, written by Origen in the third century C.E., indicates:

For who that has understanding will suppose that the first, and second, and third day, and the evening and the morning, existed without a sun, and moon, and stars? and that the first day was, as it were, also without a sky? And who is so foolish as to suppose that God, after the manner of a husbandman, planted a paradise in Eden, towards the east, and placed in it a tree of life, visible and palpable, so that one tasting of the fruit by the bodily teeth obtained life? and again, that one was a partaker of good and evil by masticating what was taken from the tree? And if God is said to walk in the paradise in the evening, and Adam to hide himself under a tree, I do not suppose that any one doubts that these things figuratively indicate certain mysteries....[11]

## PERSONAL

The conviction that God is personal has always been plainly implied both in the biblical writings and in later Jewish and Christian devotional and theological literature. In the Old Testament God speaks in personal terms (for example, "I am the God of your father, the God of Abraham, the God of Isaac, and the God of Jacob")[12] and the prophets and psalmists address God in personal terms (for example, "Hear my cry, O God, listen to my prayer.").[13] In the New Testament the same conviction of the personal character of God is embodied in the figure of fatherhood that was constantly used by Jesus as the most adequate earthly image with which to think of God.

Although belief in the Thou-hood of God thus pervades the Judaic-Christian tradition, the explicit doctrine that God is personal is of comparatively recent date, being characteristic of the theology of the nineteenth and especially of the twentieth century. In our own time the Jewish religious thinker Martin Buber has pointed to the two radically different kinds of relationship, I–Thou and I–It;[14] and a number of Christian theologians have developed the implications of the insight that God is the divine Thou who has created us as

[10]Some of the current theories about the origin of the universe are discussed in Ian Barbour, *Issues in Science and Religion* (Englewood Cliffs, N.J.: Prentice-Hall, Inc., 1966).

[11]*De Principiis*, IV, I, 16. *The Writings of the Ante-Nicene Fathers*, IV, 365.

[12]Exod. 3:6.

[13]Psalms 61:1.

[14]*I and Thou*, 1923, trans. 2nd ed. (New York: Charles Scribner's Sons, 1958).

persons in God's own image and who always deals with us in ways that respect our personal freedom and responsibility.[15] (This theme will be taken up again in the discussion of revelation and faith in Chapter 5.)

Most theologians speak of God as "personal" rather than as "a Person." The latter phrase suggests the picture of a magnified human individual. (Thinking of the divine in this way is called anthropomorphism, from the Greek *anthropos*, man, and *morphe*, shape—"in the shape of man.") The statement that God is personal is accordingly intended to signify that God is "at least personal," that whatever God may be beyond our conceiving, God is not less than personal, not a mere It, but always the higher and transcendent divine Thou.

By implication, this belief raises the question of the analogical or symbolic character of human speech about God, which will be discussed further in Chapter 7.


## LOVING, GOOD

Goodness and love are generally treated as two further attributes of God. But in the New Testament God's goodness, love, and grace are all virtually synonymous, and the most characteristic of the three terms is love.

In order to understand what the New Testament means by the love of God, it is necessary first to distinguish the two kinds of love signified by the Greek words *eros* and *agape*. *Eros* is "desiring love," love that is evoked by the desirable qualities of the beloved. This love is evoked by and depends upon the loveableness of its objects. He loves her because she is pretty, charming, cute. She loves him because he is handsome, manly, clever. Parents love their children because they are *their* children. However, when the New Testament speaks of God's love for mankind, it employs a different term, *agape*. Unlike *eros*, *agape* is unconditional and universal in its range. It is given to someone, not because she or he has special characteristics, but simply because that person is *there* as a person. The nature of *agape* is to value a person in such ways as actively to seek his or her deepest welfare and fulfillment. It is in this sense that the New Testament speaks of God's love for mankind. When it is said, for example, that "God is love"[16] or that "God so loved the world...,"[17] the word used is *agape* and its cognates.

---

[15] Among them John Oman, *Grace and Personality*, 1917 (London: Fontana Library, 1960, and New York: Association Press, 1961); Emil Brunner, *God and Man* (London: Student Christian Movement Press Ltd., 1936) and *The Divine–Human Encounter* (Philadelphia: The Westminster Press, 1942, and London: Student Christian Movement Press Ltd., 1944); H. H. Farmer, *The World and God* (Welwyn, Hertfordshire: James Nisbet & Company Ltd., 1935) and *God and Men* (Welwyn, Hertfordshire: James Nisbet & Company Ltd., 1948, and Nashville, Tenn.: Abingdon Press, 1961).

[16] I John 4:8.

[17] John 3:16.

God's universal love for human creatures, a love not rooted in their virtue or in what they have deserved but in God's own nature as *agape*, is the basis for that side of theistic religion that knows God as the final succor and security of a person's life: "God is our refuge and strength, a very present help in trouble."[18] For the ultimate of grace is believed to be also the ultimate of power, the sovereign love which guarantees our final fulfillment and well-being.

The infinite divine love also gives rise to that side of religious experience in which God is known as claiming the total obedience of a person's life. God is thought of as "Lord" and "King" as well as "Father." The divine commands come with the accent of absolute and unconditional claim, a claim that may not be set in the balance with any other interest whatever, not even life itself. This element of demand can be viewed as an expression of the divine love, seeking the best that lies potentially within the creature. Even between human beings there is nothing so inexorably demanding as a love that seeks our highest good and cannot be content that we be less than our best. Because it is infinite, the love of the Creator for the creatures made in the divine image implies a moral demand of this kind that is absolute and unqualified.

In this exposition we have subsumed the goodness of God under the love of God. But this does not avoid an important philosophical problem concerning the belief that God is good. Does that belief imply a moral standard external to God, in relation to which God can be said to be good? Or alternatively, does it mean that God is good by definition, so that God's nature, whatever it may be, is the norm of goodness?

Either position involves difficulties. If God is good in relation to some independent standard of judgment, God is no longer the sole ultimate reality, but exists in a moral universe whose character is not divinely ordained. If, however, God is good by definition, and it is a tautology that whatever God commands is right, other implications arise which are hard to accept. Suppose that, beginning tomorrow, God wills that human beings should do all the things that God has formerly willed they should not do. Now hatred, cruelty, selfishness, envy, and malice are virtues. God commands them; and since God is good, whatever God wills is right. This possibility is entailed by the view we are considering; yet it conflicts with the assumption that our present moral principles and intuitions are generally sound, or at least that they do not point us in a completely wrong direction.

Perhaps the most promising resolution of the dilemma is a frankly circular one. Good is a relational concept, referring to the fulfillment of a being's nature and basic desires. When humans call God good, they mean that God's existence and activity constitute the condition of humanity's highest good. The presupposition of such a belief is that God has made human nature in such a way that our highest fulfillment is in fact to be found in relation to God. Ethics and value theory in general are independent of religion in that their principles can be formulated without any mention of God; yet they ultimately rest upon

[18]Psalms 46:1.

the character of God, who has endowed us with the nature whose fulfillment defines our good.

In connection with the goodness of God, reference should also be made to the divine "wrath," which has played so prominent a part in religious thought. "Flee from the wrath to come" has long been the warning burden of much preaching. Some of this preaching has, ironically, embraced the very anthropomorphism which Saint Paul, whose writings supply the standard New Testament texts concerning the Wrath of God, so carefully avoided. C. H. Dodd, in his study of Saint Paul, pointed out that Paul never describes God as being wrathful, but always speaks of the Wrath of God in a curiously impersonal way to refer to the inevitable reaction of the divinely appointed moral order of the Universe upon wrongdoing. The conditions of human life are such that for an individual or a group to infringe upon the structure of the personal order is to court disaster. "This disaster Paul calls, in traditional language, 'The Wrath,' or much more rarely, 'The Wrath of God.'...' The Wrath,' then, is revealed before our eyes as the increasing horror of sin working out its hideous law of cause and effect."[19]

## HOLY

Taken separately, each of these characteristics of God, as God is conceived in the Judaic-Christian tradition, presents itself as an abstract philosophical idea. But the religious person, conscious of standing in the unseen presence of God, is overwhelmingly aware of the divine reality as infinitely other and greater. This sense of the immensity and otherness of God was expressed with unforgettable vividness by Isaiah:

> To whom then will you liken God,
>   or what likeness compare with him?
> The idol! a workman casts it,
>   and a goldsmith overlays it with gold
>   and casts for it silver chains.
> He who is impoverished chooses for an offering
>   wood that will not rot;
> he seeks out a skillful craftsman
>   to set up an image that will not move.
> Have you not known? Have you not heard?
>   Has it not been told you from the beginning?
>   Have you not understood from the foundations of the earth?
> It is he who sits above the circle of the earth,
>   and its inhabitants are like grasshoppers;

[19]C. H. Dodd, The Meaning of Paul for Today, 1920 (New York: World Publishing Company, Meridian Books, 1957), pp. 63–64.

*who stretches out the heavens like a curtain,*
   *and spreads them like a tent to dwell in;*
*who brings princes to nought,*
   *and makes the rulers of the earth as nothing...*
*To whom then will you compare me,*
   *that I should be like him? says the Holy One.*
*Lift up your eyes on high and see:*
   *who created these?[20]*

Again, God is "...the high and lofty One who inhabits eternity, whose name is Holy,"[21] whose "...thoughts are not your thoughts, neither are your ways my ways, says the Lord. For as the heavens are higher than the earth, so are my ways higher than your ways and my thoughts than your thoughts."[22] The awareness of God as holy is the awareness of One who is terrifyingly mysterious, an intensity of being in relation to which men and women are virtually nothing, a perfection in whose eyes "...all our righteousnesses are as filthy rags,"[23] a purpose and power before which we human beings can only bow down in silent awe.

We may now sum up the mainstream Judaic-Christian concept of God: God is conceived as the infinite, eternal, uncreated, personal reality, who has created all that exists and who is revealed to human creatures as holy and loving.

[20]Isa. 40:18–23, 25–26.
[21]Isa. 57:15.
[22]Isa. 55:8–9.
[23]Isa. 64:6 (King James Version).

# CHAPTER 2

# Arguments for the Existence of God

In this chapter we shall examine the most important of the philosophical arguments offered to justify belief in the reality of God. These traditional "theistic proofs" are of great philosophical interest and have been receiving more rather than less attention from both secular and religious writers in recent years.

## THE ONTOLOGICAL ARGUMENT

The ontological argument for the existence of God was first developed by Anselm, one of the Christian Church's most original thinkers and the greatest theologian ever to have been archbishop of Canterbury.[1]

Anselm begins by concentrating the monotheistic concept of God into the formula: *"a being than which nothing greater can be conceived."* It is clear that by "greater" Anselm means more perfect, rather than spatially bigger.[2] It is important to notice that the idea of the most perfect conceivable being is

[1]The ontological argument is to be found in Chaps. 2–4 of Anselm's *Proslogion*. Among the best English translations are those by M. J. Charlesworth in *St. Anselm's Proslogion* (Oxford: Clarendon Press, 1965, and University of Notre Dame Press)—from which the quotations here are taken—and Arthur C. McGill in *The Many-Faced Argument*, eds. J. H. Hick and A. C. McGill (New York: The Macmillan Company, 1967, and London: Macmillan & Company Ltd., 1968).

[2]On occasions (for example, *Proslogion*, Chaps. 14 and 18) Anselm uses "better" (*melius*) in place of "greater."

different from the idea of the most perfect being that there is. The ontological argument could not be founded upon this latter notion, for although it is true by definition that the most perfect being that there is exists, there is no guarantee that this being is what Anselm means by God. Consequently, instead of describing God as the most perfect being that there is, Anselm describes God as the being who is so perfect that no more perfect can even be conceived.

### First Form of the Argument

In the next and crucial stage of his argument Anselm distinguishes between something, $x$, existing in the mind only and its existing in reality as well. If the most perfect conceivable being existed only in the mind, we should then have the contradiction that it is possible to conceive of a yet more perfect being, namely, the same being existing in reality as well as in the mind. Therefore, the most perfect conceivable being must exist in reality as well as in the mind. Anselm's own formulation of this classic piece of philosophical reasoning is found in the second chapter of the *Proslogion*.

If then that-than-which-a-greater-cannot-be-thought exists in the mind alone, this same that-than-which-a-greater-*cannot*-be-thought is that-than-which-a-greater-*can*-be-thought. But this is obviously impossible. Therefore there is absolutely no doubt that something-than-which-a-greater-cannot-be-thought exists both in the mind and in reality.

### Second Form of the Argument

In his third chapter Anselm states the argument again, directing it now not merely to God's existence but to His uniquely *necessary* existence. God is defined in such a way that it is impossible to conceive of God's not existing. The core of this notion of necessary being is self-existence (*aseity*).[3] Since God as infinitely perfect is not limited in or by time, the twin possibilities of God's having ever come to exist or ever ceasing to exist are alike excluded and God's nonexistence is rendered impossible. The argument now runs as follows:

For something can be thought to exist that cannot be thought not to exist. Hence, if that-than-which-a-greater-cannot-be-thought can be thought not to exist, then that-than-which-a-greater-cannot-be-thought is not the same as that-than-which-a-greater-cannot-be-thought, which is absurd. Something-than-which-a-greater-cannot-be-thought exists so truly then, that it cannot be even thought not to exist.

[3]See p. 8.

## Criticisms of the Argument

In introducing the ontological argument, Anselm refers to the psalmist's "fool" who says in his heart, "There is no God."[4] Even such a person, he says, possesses the idea of God as the greatest conceivable being; and when we unpack the implications of this idea we see that such a being must actually exist. The first important critic of the argument, Gaunilon, a monk at Marmoutiers in France and a contemporary of Anselm's, accordingly entitled his reply *In Behalf of the Fool*. He claims that Anselm's reasoning would lead to absurd conclusions if applied in other fields, and he sets up a supposedly parallel ontological argument for the most perfect island. Gaunilon spoke of the most perfect of islands rather than (as he should have done) of the most perfect conceivable island; but his argument could be rephrased in terms of the latter idea. Given the idea of such an island, by using Anselm's principle we can argue that unless it exists in reality it cannot be the most perfect conceivable island!

Anselm's reply, emphasizing the uniqueness of the idea of God to show that his ontological reasoning applies only to it, is based upon the second form of the argument. The element in the idea of God which is lacking in the notion of the most perfect island is *necessary* existence. An island (or any other material object) is by definition a part of the contingent world. The most perfect island, so long as it is genuinely an island—"a piece of land surrounded by water" and thus part of the physical globe—is by definition a dependent reality, which can without contradiction be thought not to exist; and therefore Anselm's principle does not apply to it. It applies only to the most perfect conceivable being, which is defined as having eternal and independent (i.e., necessary) existence. Thus far, then, it would seem that the second form of his argument is able to withstand criticism.

Can Anselm's argument in its *first* form, however, be defended against Gaunilon's criticism? This depends upon whether the idea of the most perfect conceivable island is a coherent and consistent idea. Is it possible, even in theory, to specify the characteristics of the most perfect conceivable island? This is a question for the reader to consider.

A second phase of the debate was opened when René Descartes (1596–1650), often called the father of modern philosophy, reformulated the argument and thereby attracted widespread attention to it.[5] Descartes brought to the fore the point upon which most of the modern discussions of the onto-

---

[4]Psalms 14:1 and 53:1.

[5]*Meditations*, V. It is not entirely clear whether Descartes received the basic principle of his ontological argument from Anselm. When questioned by Mersenne about the relation of his own argument to Anselm's, he was content to reply, "I will look at St. Anselm at the first opportunity." (N. Kemp Smith, *New Studies in the Philosophy of Descartes*, London: Macmillan & Company Ltd., 1952, p. 304.) Descartes also makes another and different attempt to prove God's existence: *Discourse on Method*, IV and *Meditations*, III.

logical argument have centered, namely, the assumption that existence is a property or predicate. He explicitly treats existence as a characteristic, the possession or lack of which by a given x is properly open to inquiry. The essence or defining nature of each kind of thing includes certain predicates, and Descartes's ontological argument claims that existence must be among the defining predicates of God. Just as the fact that its internal angles are equal to two right angles is a necessary characteristic of a triangle, so existence is a necessary characteristic of a supremely perfect being. A triangle without its defining properties would not be a triangle, and God without existence would not be God. The all-important difference is that in the case of the triangle we cannot infer that any triangles exist, since existence is not of the essence of triangularity. However, in the case of a supremely perfect being we can infer existence, for existence is an essential attribute without which no being would be unlimitedly perfect.

This Cartesian version of the ontological argument was later challenged at two levels by the great German philosopher, Immanuel Kant (1724–1804).[6]

At one level he accepted Descartes's claim that the idea of existence belongs analytically to the concept of God, as the idea of having three angles belongs analytically to that of a three-sided plane figure. In each case the predicate is necessarily linked with the subject. But, Kant replied, it does not follow from this that the subject, with its predicates, actually exists. What is analytically true is that if there is a triangle, it must have three angles, and if there is an infinitely perfect being, that being must have existence. As Kant says, "To posit a triangle, and yet to reject its three angles, is self-contradictory; but there is no self-contradiction in rejecting the triangle together with its three angles. The same holds true of the concept of an absolutely necessary being."

At a deeper level, however, Kant rejected the basic assumption upon which Descartes's argument rested, the assumption that existence, like triangularity, is a predicate that something can either have or lack, and that may in some cases be analytically connected with a subject. He points out (as indeed David Hume had already pointed out in a different context)[7] that the idea of existence does not add anything to the concept of a particular thing or kind of thing. An imaginary hundred dollars, for example, consists of the same number of dollars as a real hundred dollars. When we affirm that the dollars are real, or exist, we are saying that the concept is instantiated in the world. Thus to say of x that it exists is not to say that in addition to its various other attributes it has the attribute of existing, but is to say that there is an x in the real world.

Essentially the same point has more recently been made by Bertrand Russell

[6]Immanuel Kant, *Critique of Pure Reason*, trans. N. Kemp Smith (London: Macmillan & Company Ltd., 1933, and New York: St. Martin's Press, 1969). "Transcendental Dialectic," Book II, Chap. 3, Sec. 4.

[7]David Hume, *A Treatise of Human Nature*, Book I, Part III, Sec. vii.

in his analysis of the word "exists."[8] He has shown that although "exists" is grammatically a predicate, logically it performs a different function, which can be brought out by the following translation: "Cows exist" means "There are $x$'s such that '$x$ is a cow' is true." This translation makes it clear that to say that cows exist is not to attribute a certain quality (namely existence) to cows, but is to assert that there are objects in the world to which the description summarized in the word "cow" applies. Similarly "Unicorns do not exist" is the equivalent of "There are no $x$'s such that '$x$ is a unicorn' is true." This way of construing negative existential statements—statements that deny that some particular kind of thing exists—avoids the ancient puzzle about the status of the "something" of which we assert that it does not exist. Since we can talk about unicorns, for example, it is easy to think that unicorns must in some sense be or subsist or, perhaps, that they inhabit a paradoxical realm of nonbeing or potential being. Russell's analysis, however, makes it clear that "unicorns do not exist" is not a statement about unicorns but about the concept or description "unicorn" and is the assertion that this concept has no instances.

The bearing of this upon the ontological argument is evident. If existence is, as Anselm and Descartes assumed, an attribute or predicate that can be included in a definition and that, as a desirable attribute, must be included in the definition of God, then the ontological argument is valid. For it would be self-contradictory to say that the most perfect conceivable being lacks the attribute of existence. But if existence, although it appears grammatically in the role of a predicate, has the quite different logical function of asserting that a description applies to something in reality, then the ontological argument, considered as a proof of God's existence, fails. For if existence is not a predicate, it cannot be a defining predicate of God, and the question whether anything in reality corresponds to the concept of the most perfect conceivable being remains open to inquiry. A definition of God describes one's concept of God but cannot prove the actual existence of any such being.

It should be added that some theologians, most notably Karl Barth, have seen Anselm's argument not as an attempted proof of God's existence, but as an unfolding of the significance of God's self-revelation as One whom the believer is prohibited from thinking as less than the highest conceivable reality. On this view, Anselm's argument does not seek to convert the atheist but rather to lead an already formed Christian faith into a deeper understanding of its object.[9]

---

[8]This aspect of the theory of descriptions is summarized by Russell in his *History of Western Philosophy* (London: George Allen & Unwin Ltd., 1946, and New York: Simon & Schuster), pp. 859–60. For a more technical discussion, see his *Introduction to Mathematical Philosophy* (1919), Chap. 16.

[9]See Karl Barth, *Anselm: Fides Quaerens Intellectum*, 1931 (London: Student Christian Movement Press Ltd. and Richmond, Va.: John Knox Press, 1960). Barth's interpretation is criticized by Etienne Gilson in "Sens et nature de l'argument de saint Anselme," *Archives d'histoire doctrinale et littéraire du moyen age*, 1934, pp. 23f.

The ontological argument has perennially fascinated the philosophical mind, and in recent years there have been a number of new discussions of it.[10]

## THE FIRST-CAUSE AND COSMOLOGICAL ARGUMENTS

The next important attempt to demonstrate the reality of God was that of Thomas Aquinas (1224/5–1274), who offers five ways of proving divine existence.[11] Unlike the ontological argument, which focuses attention upon the *idea* of God and proceeds to unfold its inner implications, Aquinas's proofs start from some general feature of the world around us and argue that there could not be a world with this particular characteristic unless there were also the ultimate reality which we call God. The first Way argues from the fact of change to a Prime Mover; the second from causation to a First Cause; the third from contingent beings to a Necessary Being; the fourth from degrees of value to Absolute Value; and the fifth from evidences of purposiveness in nature to a Divine Designer.

We may concentrate upon Aquinas's second and third proofs. His second proof, known as *the First-Cause argument,* is presented as follows: everything that happens has a cause, and this cause in turn has a cause, and so on in a series that must either be infinite or have its starting point in a first cause. Aquinas excludes the possibility of an infinite regress of causes and so concludes that there must be a First Cause, which we call God. (His first proof, which infers a First Mover from the fact of motion, is basically similar.)

The weakness of the argument as Aquinas states it lies in the difficulty (which he himself elsewhere acknowledges)[12] of excluding as impossible an endless regress of events, requiring no first state.

However, some contemporary Thomists (i.e., thinkers who in general follow Thomas Aquinas) have reformulated the argument in order to avoid this difficulty.[13] They interpret the endless series that it excludes, not as a regress of events back in time, but as an endless and therefore eternally inconclusive

[10]Norman Malcolm, "Anselm's Ontological Arguments," *Philosophical Review,* 1960, reprinted in *Knowledge and Certainty* (Englewood Cliffs, N.J.: Prentice-Hall, 1963). Charles Hartshorne, *The Logic of Perfection* (LaSalle, Ill.: Open Court Publishing Co., 1962), Chap. 2, and *Anselm's Discovery* (LaSalle, Ill.: Open Court Publishing Co., 1965). James F. Ross, *Philosophical Theology* (New York: Bobbs-Merrill, 1969). Alvin Plantinga, *The Nature of Necessity* (Oxford: Clarendon Press, 1974, and New York: Oxford University Press, 1979), Chap. 10, and *God, Freedom, and Evil* (London: George Allen & Unwin, Ltd., 1974, and Grand Rapids: Wm. B. Eerdmans Publishing Co., 1978), Part II.

[11]Thomas Aquinas, *Summa Theologica,* Part I, Question 2, Art. 3. For an important philosophical study of Aquinas's arguments, see Anthony Kenny, *Five Ways: St. Thomas Aquinas's Proofs of God's Existence* (London: Routledge & Kegan Paul Ltd., 1969, and Notre Dame, Ind.: University of Notre Dame Press, 1980).

[12]Aquinas, *Summa Theologica,* Part I, Question 46, Art. 2. See also *Summa Contra Gentiles,* Book II, Chap. 38

[13]For example, E. L. Mascall, *He Who Is* (London: Longmans, Green & Co., 1943), Chap. 5.

regress of explanations. If fact A is made intelligible by its relation to facts B, C, and D (which may be antecedent to or contemporary with A), and if each of these is in turn rendered intelligible by other facts, at the back of the complex there must be a reality which is self-explanatory, whose existence constitutes the ultimate explanation of the whole. If no such reality exists, the universe is a mere unintelligible brute fact.

However, this reinterpretation still leaves the argument open to two major difficulties. First, how do we know that the universe is not "a mere unintelligible brute fact"? Apart from the emotional coloring suggested by the phrase, this is precisely what the skeptic believes it to be; and to exclude this possibility at the outset is merely to beg the question at issue. The argument in effect presents the dilemma: either there is a First Cause or the universe is ultimately unintelligible; but it does not compel us to accept one horn of the dilemma rather than the other.

Second (although there is only space to suggest this difficulty, leaving the reader to develop it), the argument still depends upon a view of causality that can be, and has been, questioned. The assumption of the reformulated argument is that to indicate the causal conditions of an event is thereby to render that event intelligible. Although this assumption is true on the basis of some theories of the nature of causality, it is not true on the basis of others. For example, if (as much contemporary science assumes) causal laws state statistical probabilities,[14] or if (as Hume argued) causal connections represent mere observed sequences,[15] or are (as Kant suggested) projections of the structure of the human mind,[16] the Thomist argument fails.

Aquinas's third Way, known as the argument from the contingency of the world, and often monopolizing the name *the cosmological argument*, runs as follows. Everything in the world about us is contingent—that is, it is true of each item that it might not have existed at all or might have existed differently. The proof of this is that there was a time when it did not exist. The existence of this printed page is contingent upon the prior activities of trees, lumberjacks, transport workers, paper manufacturers, publishers, printers, author, and others, as well as upon the contemporary operation of a great number of chemical and physical laws; and each of these in turn depends upon other factors. Everything points beyond itself to other things. Saint Thomas argues that if everything were contingent, there would have been a time when nothing existed. In this case, nothing could ever have come to exist, for there would have been no causal agency. Since there are things in existence, there must therefore be something that is not contingent, and this we call God.

Aquinas's reference to a hypothetical time when nothing existed seems to

[14]Cf. Hans Reichenbach, *The Rise of Scientific Philosophy* (Berkeley: University of California Press, 1951), Chap. 10.
[15]David Hume, *An Enquiry Concerning Human Understanding*, Sec. 7.
[16]Kant, "Transcendental Analytic," in *Critique of Pure Reason*.

weaken rather than strengthen his argument, for there might be an infinite series of finite contingent events overlapping in the time sequence so that no moment occurs that is not occupied by any of them. However, modern Thomists generally omit this phase of the argument (as indeed Aquinas himself does in another book).[17] If we remove the reference to time, we have an argument based upon the logical connection between a contingent world (even if this should consist of an infinite series of events) and its noncontingent ground. One writer points as an analogy to the workings of a watch. The movement of each separate wheel and cog is accounted for by the way in which it meshes with an adjacent wheel. Nevertheless, the operation of the whole system remains inexplicable until we refer to something else outside it, namely, the spring. In order for there to be a set of interlocking wheels in movement, there must be a spring; and in order for there to be a world of contingent realities, there must be a noncontingent ground for their existence. Only a self-existent reality, containing in itself the source of its own being, can constitute an ultimate ground of the existence of anything else. Such an ultimate ground is the "necessary being" that we call God.

The most typical philosophical objection raised against this reasoning in recent years is that the idea of a "necessary being" is unintelligible. It is said that only propositions, not things, can be logically necessary, and that it is a misuse of language to speak of a logically necessary *being*.[18] This particular objection to the cosmological argument is based upon a misapprehension, for the argument does not make use of the notion of a *logically* necessary being. The concept of a necessary being used in the main theological tradition (exemplified by both Anselm and Aquinas)[19] is not concerned with logical necessity but rather with a kind of factual necessity which, in the case of God, is virtually equivalent to *aseity* or self-existence. For this reason, the idea of God's necessary being should not be equated with the view that "God exists" is a logically necessary truth.

There remains, however, an important objection to the cosmological argument, parallel to one of those applying to the First-Cause argument. The force of the cosmological form of reasoning resides in the dilemma: *either* there is a necessary being *or* the universe is ultimately unintelligible. Clearly such an argument is cogent only if the second alternative has been ruled out. Far from being ruled out, however, it represents the skeptic's position. This inability to exclude the possibility of an unintelligible universe prevents the cosmological argument from operating for the skeptic as a proof of God's existence—and the skeptic is, after all, the only person who needs such a proof.

---

[17] Aquinas, *Summa Contra Gentiles*, Book II, Chap. 15, Sec. 6.

[18] See, for example, J. J. C. Smart, "The Existence of God" and J. N. Findlay, "Can God's Existence Be Disproved?" in *New Essays in Philosophical Theology*, eds. Antony Flew and Alasdair MacIntyre (New York: The Macmillan Company and London: Student Christian Movement Press Ltd., 1955).

[19] See p. 8.

Today there is an important neo-Thomist group of thinkers who hold that there are valid forms of the cosmological argument; some of the most important writings from this point of view are listed in footnote 20.

## THE DESIGN (OR TELEOLOGICAL) ARGUMENT

This has always been the most popular of the theistic arguments, tending to evoke spontaneous assent in simple and sophisticated alike. The argument occurs in philosophical literature from Plato's *Timaeus* onward. (It appears again as the last of Saint Thomas's five Ways.) In modern times one of the most famous expositions of the argument from, or to, design is that of William Paley (1743–1805) in his *Natural Theology: or Evidences of the Existence and Attributes of the Deity Collected from the Appearances of Nature* (1802).[21] The argument is still in active commission, especially in more conservative theological circles.[22]

Paley's analogy of the watch conveys the essence of the argument. Suppose that while walking in a desert place I see a rock lying on the ground and ask myself how this object came to exist. I can properly attribute its presence to chance, meaning in this case the operation of such natural forces as wind, rain, heat, frost, and volcanic action. However, if I see a watch lying on the ground, I cannot reasonably account for it in a similar way. A watch consists of a complex arrangement of wheels, cogs, axles, springs, and balances, all operating accurately together to provide a regular measurement of the lapse of time. It would be utterly implausible to attribute the formation and assembling of these metal parts into a functioning machine to the chance operation of such factors as wind and rain. We are obliged to postulate an intelligent mind which is responsible for the phenomenon.

Paley adds certain comments that are important for his analogy between the watch and the world. First, it would not weaken our inference if we had never seen a watch before (as we have never seen a world other than this one) and therefore did not know from direct observation that watches are products of human intelligence. Second, it would not invalidate our inference from the watch to the watchmaker if we found that the mechanism did not always work

[20]Mascall, E. L., *He Who Is*, Austin Farrer, *Finite and Infinite*, 2nd ed. (London: Dacre Press, 1960). For an interesting recent presentation of the First Cause argument, appealing to current scientific cosmology, see William Lane Craig, *The Kalám Cosmological Argument* (London: Macmillan and Company Ltd. and New York: Barnes & Noble, 1979). For general treatments of cosmological arguments, see William Rowe, *The Cosmological Argument* (Princeton, N.J.: Princeton University Press, 1975) and William Lane Craig, *The Cosmological Argument from Plato to Leibniz* (London: Macmillan and New York: Barnes & Noble, 1980).

[21]Paley's book is available in an abridged version, ed. Frederick Ferré, in the Library of Liberal Arts, 1962.

[22]For example, Robert E. D. Clark, *The Universe—Plan or Accident?* (Philadelphia: Muhlenburg Press, 1961).

perfectly (as may sometimes appear to be the case with the mechanism of the world). We would still be obliged to postulate a watchmaker. Third, our inference would not be undermined if there were parts of the machine (as there are of nature) whose function we are not able to discover.

Paley argues that the natural world is as complex a mechanism, and as manifestly designed, as any watch. The rotation of the planets in the solar system and, on earth, the regular procession of the seasons and the complex structure and mutual adaptation of the parts of a living organism, all suggest design. In a human brain, for example, thousands of millions of cells function together in a coordinated system. The eye is a superb movie camera, with self-adjusting lenses, a high degree of accuracy, color sensitivity, and the capacity to operate continuously for many hours at a time. Can such complex and efficient mechanisms have come about by chance, as a stone might be formed by the random operation of natural forces?

Paley (in this respect typical of a great deal of religious apologetics in the eighteenth century) develops a long cumulative argument drawing upon virtually all the sciences of his day. As examples of divine arrangement he points to the characteristics and instincts of animals, which enable them to survive (for example, the suitability of a bird's wings to the air and of a fish's fins to the water). He is impressed by the way the alternation of day and night conveniently enables animals to sleep after a period of activity. We may conclude with an example offered by a more recent writer, who refers to the ozone layer in the atmosphere, which filters out enough of the burning ultraviolet rays of the sun to make life as we know it possible on the earth's surface. He writes:

The Ozone gas layer is a mighty proof of the Creator's forethought. Could anyone possibly attribute this device to a chance evolutionary process? A wall which prevents death to every living thing, just the right thickness, and exactly the correct defense, gives every evidence of plan.[23]

The classic critique of the design argument occurs in David Hume's *Dialogues Concerning Natural Religion*. Hume's book was published in 1779, twenty-three years earlier than Paley's; but Paley took no apparent account of Hume's criticisms—by no means the only example of lack of communication between theologians and their philosophical critics! Three of Hume's main criticisms are as follows.

1. He points out that any universe is bound to have the appearance of being designed.[24] For there could not be a universe at all in which the parts were not adapted to one another to a considerable degree. There could not, for example, be birds that grew wings but, like fish, were unable to live in the air. The

[23]Arthur I. Brown, *Footprints of God* (Findlay, Ohio: Fundamental Truth Publishers, 1943), p. 102.
[24]Hume, *Dialogues Concerning Natural Religion*, Part VIII.

persistence of any kind of life in a relatively fixed environment presupposes order and adaptation, and this can always be thought of as a deliberate product of design. The question is, however, whether this order could have come about otherwise than by conscious planning. As an alternative, Hume suggests the Epicurean hypothesis. The universe consists of a finite number of particles in random motion. In unlimited time these go through every combination that is possible to them. If one of these combinations constitutes a stable order (whether temporary or permanent), this order will in due course be realized and may be the orderly cosmos in which we now find ourselves.

This hypothesis provides a maximally simple model for a naturalistic explanation of the orderly character of the world. It can be revised and extended in the light of the special sciences. The Darwinian theory of natural selection, for example, presents a more concrete account of the apparently designed character of animal bodies. According to Darwin's theory, there are in every generation small random variations between individuals, and species are relatively well adapted to their environment for the simple reason that the less well-adapted individuals have perished in the continual competition to survive and so have not perpetuated their kind. The "struggle for survival," operating as a constant pressure toward more perfect adaptation, lies behind the evolution of life into increasingly complex forms, culminating in *homo sapiens*. To refer back to the ozone layer, the reason animal life on earth is so marvelously sheltered by this filtering arrangement is not that God first created the animals and then put the ozone layer in place to protect them, but rather that the ozone layer was there first, and only those forms of life capable of existing in the precise level of ultraviolet radiation that penetrates this layer have developed on earth.

2. The analogy between the world and a human artifact, such as a watch or a house, is rather weak.[25] The universe is not particularly like a vast machine. One could equally plausibly liken it to a great inert animal such as a crustacean, or to a vegetable. In this case the design argument fails, for whether crustaceans and vegetables are or are not consciously designed is precisely the question at issue. Only if the world is shown to be rather strikingly analogous to a human artifact, which we know to be designed, is there any basis for the inference to an intelligent Designer.

3. Even if we could validly infer a divine Designer of the world, we would still not be entitled to postulate the infinitely wise, good, and powerful God of the Judaic-Christian tradition.[26] From a given effect we can only infer a cause sufficient to produce that effect; therefore, from a finite world we can never infer an infinite creator. To use an illustration of Hume's, if I can see one side of a pair of scales and can observe that ten ounces is outweighed by

---

[25]*Dialogues*, Parts VI, VII.

[26]*Dialogues*, Part V. Cf. *An Enquiry Concerning Human Understanding*, Sec. XI, para. 105.

something on the other side, I have good evidence that the unseen object weighs more than ten ounces; however, I cannot infer from this that it weighs a hundred ounces, still less that it is infinitely heavy. On the same principle, the appearances of nature do not entitle us to affirm the existence of *one* God rather than many, since the world is full of diversity; nor of a wholly *good* God, since there is evil as well as good in the world; nor, for the same reason, of a perfectly *wise* God or an unlimitedly *powerful* one.

It has, therefore, seemed to most philosophers that the design argument, considered as a proof of the existence of God, is fatally weakened by Hume's criticisms.

## THEISM AND PROBABILITY

Since Hume's time a broader form of design argument has been offered, two generations ago by F. R. Tennant[27] and today by Richard Swinburne.[28] Both claim that when we take account of a sufficiently comprehensive range of data—not only the teleological character of biological evolution but also man's religious, moral, aesthetic, and cognitive experience[29]—it becomes cumulatively more probable that there is a God than that there is not. Theism is presented as the most probable world-view or metaphysical system.

These thinkers claim that a theistic interpretation of the world is superior to its alternatives because it alone takes adequate account of man's moral and religious experience, as well as giving due place to the material aspects of the universe. Needless to say, this claim is disputed by nontheistic thinkers, who point in particular to the existence of evil as something that fits better into a naturalistic than into a religious philosophy. The problem of evil will be discussed in Chapter 4; the question to be considered at the moment is whether the notion of probability can properly be applied to the rival hypotheses of the existence and nonexistence of God.

Two main theories of probability, the "frequency" theory and the "reasonableness of belief" theory, are found in contemporary writings on the subject, developing what are sometimes called the statistical and inductive senses of probability. According to the first, probability is a statistical concept, of use only where there is a plurality of cases.[30] (For example, since a die has six faces, each of which is equally likely to fall uppermost, the probability of throwing

[27]F. R. Tennant, *Philosophical Theology*, II (Cambridge: Cambridge University Press, 1930), Chap. 4.

[28]Richard Swinburne, *The Existence of God* (London and New York: Oxford University Press, 1979).

[29]Richard Taylor in *Metaphysics*, 3rd ed. (Englewood Cliffs, N.J.: Prentice-Hall, Inc., 1983), Chap. 7, makes striking use of man's cognitive experience in a reformulated design argument.

[30]See, for example, Morris R. Cohen, *A Preface to Logic* (London: Routledge & Kegan Paul Ltd., 1946, and New York: Dover Publications, Inc., 1944), Chap. 6.

any one particular number at a given throw is one in six.) As David Hume points out, the fact that there is only one universe precludes our making probable judgments of this kind about it. If—impossibly—we knew that there were a number of universes (for example, ten) and if in addition we knew that, say, half of them were God-produced and half not, then we could deduce that the probability of our own universe's being God-produced would be one in two. However, since by "the universe" we mean the totality of all that is (other than any creator of the universe), clearly no reasoning based upon the frequency theory of probability is possible concerning its character.

According to the other type of probability theory, to say that statement $p$ is more probable than statement $q$ is to say that when they are both considered in relation to a common body of prior (evidence-stating) propositions, it is more "reasonable" to believe $p$ than $q$, or $p$ is more worthy of belief than $q$.[31] The definition of reasonableness of course presents problems; but there is another special difficulty that hinders the use of this concept to assess the "theous" or "nontheous" character of the universe. In the unique case of the universe as a whole there is no body of prior evidence-stating propositions to which we can appeal, since all our propositions must be about either the whole or a part of the universe itself. In other words, there is nothing outside the universe that might count as evidence concerning its nature. There is only one universe, and this one and only universe is capable of being interpreted both theistically and nontheistically.

It has been suggested that we may speak of "alogical" probabilities and may claim that in a sense that operates in everyday common-sense judgments, although this is not capable of being mathematically formulated, it is more likely or probable that there is than that there is not a God.[32] According to this view, the considerations that support the God hypothesis are entitled to greater weight than those that suggest the contrary hypothesis. This, however, is clearly a question-begging procedure, for there are no common scales on which to weigh, for example, the human sense of moral obligation against the reality of evil, or humanity's religious experience against the fact of human iniquity. Nor does there seem to be any valid sense in which it can be said that a religious interpretation of life is *antecedently* more probable than a naturalistic interpretation, or vice versa. Since we are dealing with a unique phenomenon, the category of probability has no proper application to it.

On the other hand, Richard Swinburne has recently argued that the theistic explanation of the character of the universe is the simplest and most comprehensive available and can be shown by use of Bayes's theorem to have an overall probability greater than one-half. His argument is fascinating and

[31]See, for example, Roderick M. Chisholm, *Perceiving* (Ithaca, N.Y.: Cornell University Press, 1957), Chap. 2.
[32]See, for example, Tennant, *Philosophical Theology*, I, Chap. 11.

complex, but has also been seriously criticized, and provides a good topic for the more advanced student to pursue.[33]

## THE MORAL ARGUMENT

The moral argument, in its various forms, claims that ethical experience, and particularly one's sense of an inalienable obligation to one's fellow human beings, presupposes the reality of God as in some way the source and ground of this obligation.

### First Form

In one form the argument is presented as a logical inference from objective moral laws to a divine Law Giver; or from the objectivity of moral values or of values in general to a transcendent Ground of Values; or again, from the fact of conscience to a God whose "voice" conscience is—as in the following passage by Cardinal Newman:

If, as is the case, we feel responsibility, are ashamed, are frightened, at transgressing the voice of conscience, this implies that there is One to whom we are responsible, before whom we are ashamed, whose claims upon us we fear....If the cause of these emotions does not belong to this visible world, the Object to which [the conscientious person's] perception is directed must be Supernatural and Divine.[34]

The basic assumption of all arguments of this kind is that moral values are not capable of naturalistic explanation in terms of human needs, desires and ideals, self-interest, the structure of human nature or human society, or in any other way that does not involve appeal to the Supernatural. But to make such an assumption is to beg the question. Thus, an essential premise of the inference from axiology to God is in dispute, and from the point of view of the naturalistic skeptic nothing has been established.

### Second Form

The second kind of moral argument is not open to the same objection, for it is not strictly a proof at all. It consists of the claim that anyone seriously committed to respect moral values as exercising a sovereign claim upon his or her life must thereby implicitly believe in the reality of a transhuman source and basis for these values, which religion calls God. Thus, Immanuel Kant

---

[33]Swinburne's argument occurs in his *The Existence of God*. It is criticized in, for example, John Hick, *An Interpretation of Religion* (New Haven: Yale University Press and London: Macmillan, 1989), Chap. 4.

[34]J. H. Cardinal Newman, *A Grammar of Assent*, 1870, ed. C. F. Harrold (New York: David McKay Co., Inc., 1947), pp. 83–84.

argues that both immortality and the existence of God are "postulates" of the moral life, i.e., beliefs which can legitimately be affirmed as presuppositions by one who recognizes duty as rightfully laying upon one an unconditional claim.[35] Again, a more recent theological writer asks:

Is it too paradoxical in the modern world to say that faith in God is a very part of our moral consciousness, without which the latter becomes meaningless?...Either our moral values tell us something about the nature and purpose of reality (i.e., give us the germ of religious belief) or they are subjective and therefore meaningless.[36]

It seems to the present writer that so long as this contention is not overstated it has a certain limited validity. To recognize moral claims as taking precedence over all other interests is, implicitly, to believe in a reality of some kind, other than the natural world, that is superior to oneself and entitled to one's obedience. This is at least a move in the direction of belief in God, who is known in the Judaic-Christian tradition as the supreme moral reality. But it cannot be presented as a proof of God's existence, for the sovereign authority of moral obligation can be questioned; and even if moral values are acknowledged as pointing toward a transcendent ground, they cannot be said to point all the way to the infinite, omnipotent, self-existent, personal creator who is the object of biblical faith.

---

[35]*Critique of Practical Reason*, Book II, Chap. 2, Secs. 4 and 5.

[36]D. M. Baillie, *Faith in God and Its Christian Consummation* (Edinburgh: T. & T. Clark, 1927), pp. 172–73.

# CHAPTER 3

# Arguments Against the Existence of God

The responsible skeptic, whether agnostic or atheist, is not concerned to deny that religious people have had certain experiences as a result of which they have become convinced of the reality of God. The skeptic believes, however, that these experiences can be adequately accounted for without postulating a God and by adopting instead a naturalistic interpretation of religion. Two of the most influential such interpretations will now be discussed.

## THE SOCIOLOGICAL THEORY OF RELIGION

Developed earlier in the present century mainly by French sociologists, principally Emile Durkheim,[1] this type of analysis appeals today to a generation that is acutely conscious of the power of society to mold for good or ill the minds of its members.

The sociological theory refers to this power when it suggests that the gods whom people worship are imaginary beings unconsciously fabricated by society as instruments whereby society exercises control over the thoughts and behavior of the individual.

The theory claims that when men and women have the religious feeling of standing before a higher power that transcends their personal lives and

[1]*The Elementary Forms of the Religious Life*, 1912 (London: George Allen & Unwin Ltd., 1915, and New York: The Free Press, 1965).

impresses its will upon them as a moral imperative, they are indeed in the presence of a greater environing reality. This reality is not, however, a supernatural Being; it is the natural fact of society. The encompassing human group exercises the attributes of deity in relation to its members and gives rise in their minds to the idea of God, which is thus, in effect, a symbol for society.

The sense of the holy, and of God as the source of sacred demand claiming the total allegiance of the worshiper, is thus accounted for as a reflection of society's absolute claim upon the loyalty of its members. In the Australian aboriginal societies, in relation to which Durkheim's theory was originally worked out, this sense of the group's right to unquestioning obedience and loyalty was very strong. The tribe or clan was a psychic organism within which the human members lived as cells, not yet fully separated out as individuals from the group mind. Its customs, beliefs, requirements, and taboos were sovereign and had collectively the awesome aspect of the holy. In advanced societies this primitive unity has enjoyed a partial revival in time of war, when the national spirit has been able to assert an almost unlimited authority over the citizens.

The key to the complementary sense of God as people's final succor and security is found, according to Durkheim, in the way in which the individual is carried and supported in all the major crises of life by the society to which he or she belongs. We humans are social to the roots of our being and are deeply dependent upon our group and unhappy when isolated from it. It is a chief source of our psychic vitality, and we draw strength and reinforcement from it when as worshipers we celebrate with our fellows the religion that binds us together ("religion" probably derives from the Latin *ligare*, to bind or bind together.)

It is, then, society as a greater environing reality standing over against the individual, a veritable "ancient of days" existing long before one's little life and destined to persist long after one's disappearance, that constitutes the concrete reality which has become symbolized as God. This theory accounts for the transformation of the natural pressures of society into the felt supernatural presence of God by referring to a universal tendency of the human mind to create mental images and symbols.

Here, in brief, is an interpretation of the observable facts of religion that involves no reference to God as a supernatural Being who has created humanity and the world in which we live. According to this interpretation, it is, on the contrary, the human animal who has created God in order to preserve its own social existence.

Religious thinkers have offered various criticisms of this theory, the following difficulties being stressed:[2]

[2]For example, by H. H. Farmer, *Towards Belief in God* (London: Student Christian Movement Press Ltd., 1942), Chap. 9, to which the present discussion is indebted.

1. It is claimed that the theory fails to account for the universal reach of the religiously informed conscience, which on occasion goes beyond the boundaries of any empirical society and acknowledges a moral relationship to human beings as such. In the understanding of the great teachers of the monotheistic faiths, the corollary of monotheism has been pressed home: God loves *all* human beings and summons *all* men and women to care for one another as brothers and sisters.

How is this striking phenomenon to be brought within the scope of the sociological theory? If the call of God is only society imposing upon its members forms of conduct that are in the interest of that society, what is the origin of the obligation to be concerned equally for *all* humanity? The human race as a whole is not a society as the term is used in the sociological theory. How, then, can the voice of God be equated with that of the group if this voice impels one to extend equally to outsiders the jealously guarded privileges of the group?

2. It is claimed that the sociological theory fails to account for the moral creativity of the prophetic mind. The moral prophet is characteristically an innovator who goes beyond the established ethical code and summons his or her fellows to acknowledge new and more far-reaching claims of morality upon their lives. How is this to be accounted for if there is no other source of moral obligation than the experience of the organized group intent upon its own preservation and enhancement? The sociological theory fits a static "closed society," but how can it explain the ethical progress that has come about through the insights of pioneers morally in advance of their groups?

3. It is claimed that the sociological theory fails to explain the socially detaching power of conscience. Again the criticism focuses upon the individual who is set at variance with society because he or she "marches to a different drum"—for example, an Amos denouncing the Hebrew society of his time or, to span the centuries, a Trevor Huddlestone or Beyers Naudé rejecting the hegemony of their own race in South Africa, or Camilo Torres in Colombia, or Vietnam War resisters. If the sociological theory is correct, the sense of divine support should be at a minimum or even altogether absent in such cases. How can the prophet have the support of God against society if God is simply society in disguise? The record shows, however, that the sense of divine backing and support is often at a maximum in such situations. These people are sustained by a vivid sense of the call and leadership of the Eternal. It is striking that in one instance after another the Hebrew prophets express a sense of closeness to God as they are rejected by their own people; yet they belonged to an intensely self-conscious and nationalistic society of the kind that, according to the sociological theory, ought most readily to be best able to impress its will upon its members.

It seems, then, that a verdict of "not proven" is indicated concerning this attempt to establish a purely natural explanation of religion.

## THE FREUDIAN THEORY OF RELIGION

Sigmund Freud (1856–1939), the originator of psychoanalysis and a figure comparable in importance to Galileo, Darwin, or Einstein, devoted a good deal of attention to the nature of religion.[3] He regarded religious beliefs as "...illusions, fulfillments of the oldest, strongest, and most insistent wishes of mankind."[4] Religion, as Freud saw it, is a mental defense against the more threatening aspects of nature—earthquake, flood, storm, disease, and inevitable death. According to Freud, "With these forces nature rises up against us, majestic, cruel and inexorable."[5] But the human imagination transforms these forces into mysterious personal powers.[6]

Impersonal forces and destinies [Freud said] cannot be approached; they remain eternally remote. But if the elements have passions that rage as they do in our own souls, if death itself is not something spontaneous but the violent act of an evil Will, if everywhere in nature there are Beings around us of a kind that we know in our own society, then we can breathe freely, can feel at home in the uncanny and can deal by psychical means with our senseless anxiety. We are still defenseless, perhaps, but we are no longer helplessly paralyzed; we can at least react. Perhaps, indeed, we are not even defenseless. We can apply the same methods against these violent super beings outside that we employ in our own society; we can try to adjure them, to appease them, to bribe them, and, by so influencing them, we may rob them of part of their power.

The solution adopted in Judaic-Christian religion is to project upon the universe the buried memory of our father as a great protecting power. The face that smiled at us in the cradle, now magnified to infinity, smiles down upon us from heaven. Thus, religion is "...the universal obsessional neurosis of humanity,"[7] which may be left behind when at last people learn to face the world, relying no longer upon illusions but upon scientifically authenticated knowledge.

In *Totem and Taboo*, Freud uses his distinctive concept of the Oedipus complex[8] (which rests on concurrent ambivalent feelings) to account for the tremendous emotional intensity of religious life and the associated feelings of guilt and of obligation to obey the behests of the deity. He postulates a stage

---

[3]See his *Totem and Taboo* (1913), *The Future of an Illusion* (1927), *Moses and Monotheism* (1939), *The Ego and the Id* (1923), and *Civilization and Its Discontents* (1930).

[4]*The Future of an Illusion. The Complete Psychological Works of Sigmund Freud*, trans. and ed. James Strachey (New York: Liveright Corporation and London: The Hogarth Press Ltd., 1961), XXI, 30.

[5]*Ibid.*, 16.

[6]*Ibid.*, 16–17.

[7]*Ibid.*, 44.

[8]Oedipus is a figure in Greek mythology who unknowingly killed his father and married his mother; the Oedipus complex of Freudian theory is the child's unconscious jealousy of his father and desire for his mother.

of human prehistory in which the unit was the "primal horde" consisting of father, mother, and offspring. The father, as the dominant male, retained to himself exclusive rights over the females and drove away or killed any of the sons who challenged his position. Finding that individually they could not defeat the father-leader, the sons eventually banded together to kill (and also, being cannibals, to eat) him. This was the primal crime, the patricide that has set up tensions within the human psyche out of which have developed moral inhibitions, totemism, and the other phenomena of religion. For having slain their father, the brothers are struck with remorse. They also find that they cannot all succeed to his position and that there is a continuing need for restraint. The dead father's prohibition accordingly takes on a new ("moral") authority as a taboo against incest. This association of religion with the Oedipus complex, which is renewed in each male individual,[9] is held to account for the mysterious authority of God in the human mind and the powerful guilt feelings which make people submit to such a fantasy. Religion is thus a "return of the repressed."

There is an extensive literature discussing the Freudian treatment of religion, which cannot, however, be summarized here.[10] The "primal horde" hypothesis, which Freud took over from Darwin and Robertson Smith, is now generally rejected by anthropologists,[11] and the Oedipus complex itself is no longer regarded, even by many of Freud's successors, as the key to unlock all doors. Philosophical critics have further pointed out that Freud's psychic atomism and determinism have the status not of observational reports but of philosophical theories.

Although Freud's account of religion, taken as a whole, is highly speculative and will probably be the least-enduring aspect of his thought, his general view that faith is a kind of "psychological crutch" and has the quality of fantasy thinking is endorsed by many internal as well as external critics as applying

---

[9]Freud seems to have regarded religion as a male creation, which has been secondarily imposed upon women.

[10]Some of the discussions from the side of theology are: Ian Suttie, *The Origins of Love and Hate* (London: Kegan Paul, 1935); R. S. Lee, *Freud and Christianity* (London: James Clarke Co. Ltd., 1948); H. L. Philip, *Freud and Religious Belief* (London: Rockliff, 1956, and Westport, Conn.: Greenwood Press, 1974); Arthur Guirdham, *Christ and Freud* (London: George Allen & Unwin Ltd., 1959); and from the side of psychoanalytic theory, T. Reik, *Dogma and Compulsion* (New York: International Universities Press, 1951); M. Ostow and B. Scharfstein, *The Need to Believe* (New York: International Universities Press, 1954); J. C. Flugel, *Man, Morals, and Society* (New York: International Universities Press, 1947).

[11]A. L. Kroeber, *Anthropology*, rev. ed. (New York: Harcourt Brace Jovanovich, Inc., 1948), p. 616. Kroeber describes the psychoanalytic explanation of culture as "intuitive, dogmatic, and wholly unhistorical." Bronislaw Malinowski remarks in the course of a careful examination of Freud's theory, "It is easy to perceive that the primeval horde has been equipped with all the bias, maladjustments and ill-tempers of a middle-class European family, and then let loose in a prehistoric jungle to run riot in a most attractive but fantastic hypothesis." Bronislaw Malinowski, *Sex and Repression in Savage Society* (London: Routledge & Kegan Paul Ltd., 1927, and New York: Humanities Press, 1953), p. 165.

to much that is popularly called religion. Empirical religion is a bewildering mixture of elements, and undoubtedly wish fulfillment enters in and is a major factor in the minds of many devotees.

Perhaps the most interesting theological comment to be made upon Freud's theory is that in his work on the father-image he may have uncovered one of the mechanisms by which God creates an idea of deity in the human mind. For if the relation of a human father to his children is, as the Judaic-Christian tradition teaches, analogous to God's relationship to humanity, it is not surprising that human beings should think of God as their heavenly Father and should come to know God through the infant's experience of utter dependence and the growing child's experience of being loved, cared for, and disciplined within a family. Clearly, to the mind that is not committed in advance to a naturalistic explanation there may be a religious as well as a naturalistic interpretation of the psychological facts.

Again, then, it seems that the verdict must be "not proven"; like the sociological theory, the Freudian theory of religion *may* be true but has not been shown to be so.


## THE CHALLENGE OF MODERN SCIENCE

The tremendous expansion of scientific knowledge in the modern era has had a profound influence upon religious belief. Further, this influence has been at a maximum within the Judaic-Christian tradition, with which we are largely concerned in this book. There have been a series of specific jurisdictional disputes between the claims of scientific and religious knowledge, and also a more general cumulative effect which constitutes a major factor, critical of religion, in the contemporary intellectual climate.

Since the Renaissance, scientific information about the world has steadily expanded in fields such as astronomy, geology, zoology, chemistry, biology, and physics; and contradicting assertions in the same fields, derived from the Bible rather than from direct observation and experiment, have increasingly been discarded. In each of the great battles between scientists and church people the validity of the scientific method was vindicated by its practical fruitfulness. Necessary adjustments were eventually made in the aspects of religious belief that had conflicted with the scientists' discoveries. As a result of this long debate it has become apparent that the biblical writers, recording their experience of God's activity in human history, inevitably clothed their testimony in their own contemporary prescientific understanding of the world. Advancing knowledge has made it necessary to distinguish between their record of the divine presence and calling, and the primitive world view that formed the framework of their thinking. Having made this distinction, the modern reader can learn to recognize the aspects of the scriptures that reflect the prescientific culture prevailing at the human end of any divine-human encounter. Accordingly, we find that the three-storied universe of biblical cosmology, with heaven in the sky above our heads, hell in the ground beneath our feet, and the sun circling the earth but halting in its course at Joshua's command, is no longer credible in the light of modern knowledge. That the world was created some 6,000 years ago and that humanity and the other animal species came into being at that time in their present forms can no longer be regarded as a reasonable belief. Again, the expectation that at some future date the decomposed corpses of humanity through the ages will rise from the earth in pristine health for judgment has largely ceased to be entertained. Yet, in all of these cases, church members initially resisted, often with great vehemence and passion, the scientific evidence that conflicted with their customary beliefs.[12] In part, this resistance represented the natural reaction of conservative-minded people who preferred established and familiar scientific theories to new and disturbing ones. But this reaction was supported and reinforced by an unquestioning acceptance of the propositional conception of revelation (see pp. 56–58). This conception assumes that all statements in the scriptures are God's statements; consequently, to question any of them is either to accuse God of lying or to deny that the Bible is divinely inspired.

The more general legacy of this long history of interlocking scientific advance and theological retreat is the assumption, now part of the climate of thought in our twentieth-century Western world, that even though the sciences have not specifically disproved the claims of religion, they have thrown such a flood of light upon the world (without at any point encountering that of which religion speaks) that faith can now be regarded as a harmless private fantasy. Religion is seen as a losing cause, destined to be ousted from more and more areas of human knowledge until at last it arrives at a status akin to that of astrology—a cultural "fifth wheel," persisting only as a survival from previous ages in which our empirical knowledge was much less developed.

The sciences have cumulatively established the autonomy of the natural order. From the galaxies whose vastness numbs the mind to the unimaginably small events and entities of the subatomic universe, and throughout the endless complexities of our own world, which lies between these virtual infinities, nature can be studied without any reference to God. The universe investigated by the sciences proceeds exactly as though no God exists.

Does it follow from this fact that there is, indeed, no God?

There are forms of theistic belief from which this negative conclusion follows and others from which it does not.

If belief in the reality of God is tied to the cultural presuppositions of a prescientific era, this set of beliefs, taken as a whole, is no longer valid. But the situation is otherwise if we suppose (with much contemporary theology) that

---

[12]The classic history of these battles is found in A. D. White, *A History of the Warfare of Science with Theology* (1896), 2 vols., available in a paperback edition (New York: Dover Publications, Inc., 1960).

God has created this universe, insofar as its creation relates to humanity, as a neutral sphere in which we are endowed with a sufficient degree of autonomy to be able to enter into a freely accepted relationship with our Maker. From this point of view, God maintains a certain distance from us, a certain margin for a creaturely independence which, although always relative and conditioned, is nevertheless adequate for our existence as responsible persons. This "distance" is epistemic rather than spatial. It consists of the circumstance that God, being not inescapably evident to the human mind, is known only by means of an uncompelled response of faith.[13] This circumstance requires that the human environment should have the kind of autonomy that, in fact, we find it to have. It must constitute a working system capable of being investigated indefinitely without the investigator's being driven to postulate God as an element within it or behind it. From the point of view of this conception of God, the autonomy of nature, as it is increasingly confirmed by the sciences, offers no contradiction to religious faith. The sciences are exploring a universe that is divinely created and sustained, but with its own God-given autonomy and integrity. Such an understanding of God and of the divine purpose for the world is able to absorb scientific discoveries, both accomplished and projected, that had initially seemed to many religious believers to be profoundly threatening. The tracing back of our continuity with the animal kingdom; the locating of the origin of organic life in natural chemical reactions taking place on the earth's surface, with the consequent prospect of one day reproducing these reactions in the laboratory; the exploration of outer space and the possibility of encountering advanced forms of life on other planets; the probing of the chemistry of personality and the perfecting of the sinister techniques of "brainwashing"; the contemporary biomedical revolution, creating new possibilities for the control of the human genetic material through, for example, gene deletion and cloning; the harnessing of nuclear energy and the dread possibility of human self-destruction in a nuclear war—all these facts and possibilities, with their immense potentialities for good and evil, are aspects of a natural order that possesses its own autonomous structure. According to religious faith, God created this order as an environment in which human beings, living as free and responsible agents, might enter into a relationship with God. All that can be said about the bearing of scientific knowledge upon this religious claim is that it does not fall within the province of any of the special sciences: science can neither confirm nor deny it.

From this theological point of view, what is the status of the miracle stories and the accounts of answered prayer that abound in the scriptures and in human records from the earliest to the present time? Must these be considered incompatible with a recognition that an autonomous natural order is the proper province of the sciences?

---

[13]For further elaboration of this idea see pp. 64–65. For a contrary point of view see Robert Mesle, "Does God Hide From Us?" *The International Journal for Philosophy of Religion*, vol. 24 (1988)

The answer to this question depends upon how we define "miracle." It is possible to define the term in either purely physical and nonreligious terms, as a breach or suspension of natural law, or in religious terms, as an unusual and striking event that evokes and mediates a vivid awareness of God. If "miracle" is defined as a breach of natural law, one can declare *a priori* that there are no miracles. It does not follow, however, that there are no miracles in the religious sense of the term, for the principle that nothing happens in conflict with natural law does not entail that there are no unusual and striking events evoking and mediating a vivid awareness of God. Natural law consists of generalizations formulated retrospectively to cover whatever has, in fact, happened. When events take place that are not covered by the generalizations accepted thus far, the properly scientific response is not to deny that they occurred but to seek to revise and extend the current understanding of nature in order to include them. Without regard to the relevant evidence, it cannot be said that the story, for example, of Jesus's healing the man with the withered hand (Luke 6:6–11) is untrue, or that comparable stories from later ages or from the present day are untrue. It is not scientifically impossible that unusual and striking events of this kind have occurred. Events with religious significance, evoking and mediating a vivid sense of the presence and activity of God, may have occurred, even though their continuity with the general course of nature cannot be traced in the present very limited state of human knowledge.

In the religious apologetic of former centuries miracles have played an important part. They have been supposed to empower religion to demand and compel belief. In opposition to this traditional view many theologians today believe that, far from providing the foundation of religious faith, miracles presuppose such faith. The religious response, which senses the purpose of God in the inexplicable coincidence or the improbable and unexpected occurrence, constitutes an event a miracle. Thus miracles belong to the internal life of a community of faith; they are not the means by which it can seek to evangelize the world outside.[14]

The conclusion of this chapter is thus parallel to the conclusion of the preceding one. There it appeared that we cannot decisively prove the existence of God; here it appears that neither can we decisively disprove God's existence. We have yet to consider what is, for many people, the most powerful reason for doubting the reality of a loving God, namely the immense weight both of human suffering and of human wickedness. This is so important an issue that the entire next chapter will be devoted to it.

[14]One of the best modern treatments of miracles is found in H. H. Farmer, *The World and God: A Study of Prayer, Providence and Miracle in Christian Experience,* 2nd ed. (London: Nisbet & Co., 1936). See also C. S. Lewis, *Miracles: A Preliminary Study* (London: The Centenary Press, 1947, and New York: Macmillan Publishing Co., 1963).

# CHAPTER 4

# The Problem of Evil

## THE PROBLEM

For many people it is, more than anything else, the appalling depth and extent of human suffering, together with the selfishness and greed which produce so much of this, that makes the idea of a loving Creator seem implausible and disposes them toward one of the various naturalistic theories of religion.

Rather than attempt to define "evil" in terms of some theological theory (for example, as "that which is contrary to God's will"), it seems better to define it ostensively, by indicating that to which the word refers. It refers to physical pain, mental suffering, and moral wickedness. The last is one of the causes of the first two, for an enormous amount of human pain arises from people's inhumanity. This pain includes such major scourges as poverty, oppression and persecution, war, and all the injustice, indignity, and inequity that have occurred throughout history. Even disease is fostered, to an extent that has not yet been precisely determined by psychosomatic medicine, by emotional and moral factors seated both in individuals and in their social environment. However, although a great deal of pain and suffering are caused by human action, there is yet more that arises from such natural causes as bacteria and earthquakes, storm, fire, lightning, flood, and drought.

As a challenge to theism, the problem of evil has traditionally been posed in the form of a dilemma: if God is perfectly loving, God must wish to abolish all evil; and if God is all-powerful, God must be able to abolish all evil. But evil exists; therefore God cannot be both omnipotent and perfectly loving.

One possible solution (offered, for example, by contemporary Christian Science) can be ruled out immediately so far as the traditional Judaic-Christian faith is concerned. To say that evil is an illusion of the human mind is impossible within a religion based upon the stark realism of the Bible. Its pages faithfully reflect the characteristic mixture of good and evil in human experience. They record every kind of sorrow and suffering, every mode of "man's inhumanity to man" and of our painfully insecure existence in the world. There is no attempt to regard evil as anything but dark, menacingly ugly, heartrending, and crushing. There can be no doubt, then, that for biblical faith evil is entirely real and in no sense an illusion.

There are three main Christian responses to the problem of evil: the Augustinian response, hinging upon the concept of the fall of man from an original state of righteousness; the Irenaean response, hinging upon the idea of the gradual creation of a perfected humanity through life in a highly imperfect world; and the response of modern process theology, hinging upon the idea of a God who is not all-powerful and not in fact able to prevent the evils arising either in human beings or in the processes of nature.

Before examining each of these three responses, or theodicies,[1] we will discuss a position that is common to all of them.

The common ground is some form of what has come to be called the free-will defense, at least so far as the moral evil of human wickedness is concerned, for Christian thought has always seen moral evil as related to human freedom and responsibility. To be a person is to be a finite center of freedom, a (relatively) self-directing agent responsible for one's own decisions. This involves being free to act wrongly as well as rightly. There can therefore be no certainty in advance that a genuinely free moral agent will never choose amiss. Consequently, according to the strong form of free-will defense, the possibility of wrongdoing is logically inseparable from the creation of finite persons, and to say that God should not have created beings who might sin amounts to saying that God should not have created people.

This thesis has been challenged by those who claim that no contradiction is involved in saying that God might have made people who would be genuinely free but who could at the same time be guaranteed always to act rightly. To quote from one of these:

If there is no logical impossibility in a man's freely choosing the good on one, or on several occasions, there cannot be a logical impossibility in his freely choosing the good on every occasion. God was not, then, faced with a choice between making innocent automata and making beings who, in acting freely, would sometimes go wrong: there

---

[1] "Theodicy," formed (by Leibniz) from the Greek *theos*, god, and *dike*, righteous, is a technical term for attempts to solve the theological problem of evil.

was open to him the obviously better possibility of making beings who would act freely but always go right. Clearly, his failure to avail himself of this possibility is inconsistent with his being both omnipotent and wholly good.[2]

This argument has considerable power. A modified form of free-will defense has, however, been suggested in response to it. If by free actions we mean actions that are not externally compelled, but flow from the nature of agents as they react to the circumstances in which they find themselves, then there is indeed no contradiction between our being free and our actions' being "caused" (by our own God-given nature) and thus being in principle predictable. However, it is suggested, there is a contradiction in saying that *God* is the cause of our acting as we do *and* that we are free beings specifically in relation to God. The contradiction is between holding that God has so made us that we shall of necessity act in a certain way, and that we are genuinely independent persons *in relation to God*. If all our thoughts and actions are divinely predestined, then however free and responsible we may seem to ourselves to be, we are not free and responsible in the sight of God but must instead be God's puppets. Such "freedom" would be comparable to that of patients acting out a series of posthypnotic suggestions: they appear to themselves to be free, but their volitions have actually been predetermined by the will of the hypnotist, in relation to whom the patients are therefore not genuinely free agents. Thus, it is suggested, while God *could* have created such beings, there would have been no point in doing so—at least not if God is seeking to create sons and daughters rather than human puppets.

## THE AUGUSTINIAN THEODICY

The main traditional Christian response to the problem of evil was formulated by St. Augustine (354–430 A.D.) and has constituted the majority report of the Christian mind through the centuries, although it has been much criticized in recent times. It includes both philosophical and theological strands. The main philosophical position is the idea of the negative or privative nature of evil. Augustine holds firmly to the Hebrew-Christian conviction that the universe is *good*—that is to say, it is the creation of a good God for a good purpose. There are, according to Augustine, higher and lower, greater and lesser goods in immense abundance and variety; however, everything that has being is good in its own way and degree, except insofar as it has become spoiled or

---

[2]J. L. Mackie, "Evil and Omnipotence," *Mind* (April 1955), p. 209. A similar point is made by Antony Flew in "Divine Omnipotence and Human Freedom," *New Essays in Philosophical Theology*. An important critical comment on these arguments is offered by Ninian Smart in "Omnipotence, Evil and Supermen," *Philosophy* (April 1961), with replies by Flew (January 1962) and Mackie (April 1962). See also Alvin Plantinga, *God, Freedom and Evil* (Grand Rapids: Wm. B. Eerdmans Publishing Co., 1977).

corrupted. Evil—whether it be an evil will, an instance of pain, or some disorder or decay in nature—has therefore not been set there by God but represents the going wrong of something that is inherently good. Augustine points to blindness as an example. Blindness is not a "thing." The only thing involved is the eye, which is in itself good; the evil of blindness consists of the lack of a proper functioning of the eye. Generalizing the principle, Augustine holds that evil always consists of the malfunctioning of something that is in itself good.

As it originally came forth from the hand of God, then, the universe was a perfect harmony expressing the creative divine intention. It was a graded hierarchy of higher and lower forms of being, each good in its own place. How, then, did evil come about? It came about initially in those levels of the universe that involve free will: the free will of the angels and of human beings. Some of the angels turned from the supreme Good, which is God, to lesser goods, thereby rebelling against their creator; they in turn tempted the first man and woman to fall. This fall of angelic and human beings was the origin of moral evil or sin. The natural evils of disease, of "nature red in tooth and claw," and of earthquake, storm, and so on are the penal consequences of sin, for humanity was intended to be guardian of the earth, and this human defection has set all nature awry. Thus Augustine could say, "All evil is either sin or the punishment for sin."[3]

The Augustinian theodicy adds that at the end of history there will come the judgment, when many will enter into eternal life and many others (who in their freedom have rejected God's offer of salvation) into eternal torment. For Augustine, "since there is happiness for those who do not sin, the universe is perfect; and it is no less perfect because there is misery for sinners...the penalty of sin corrects the dishonour of sin."[4] He is invoking here a principle of moral balance according to which sin that is justly punished is thereby cancelled out and no longer regarded as marring the perfection of God's universe.

The Augustinian theodicy fulfills the intention lying behind it, which is to clear the creator of any responsibility for the existence of evil by loading that responsibility without remainder upon the creature. Evil stems from the culpable misuse of creaturely freedom in a tragic act, of cosmic significance, in the prehistory of the human race—an act that was prefigured in the heavenly realms by the incomprehensible fall of some of the angels, the chief of whom is now Satan, God's Enemy.

This theodicy has been criticized in the modern period, the first major critic being the great German Protestant theologian Friedrich Schleiermacher (1768–1834).[5]

---

[3]*De Genesi Ad Litteram*, Imperfectus liber, 1.3.

[4]*On Free Will*, III, ix. 26.

[5]See Schleiermacher's *The Christian Faith*, Second Part, "Explication of the Consciousness of Sin."

The basic criticism is directed at the idea that a universe which God has created with absolute power, so as to be exactly as God wishes it to be, containing no evil of any kind, has nevertheless gone wrong. It is true that the free creatures who are part of it are free to fall. However, since they are finitely perfect, without any taint or trace of evil in them, and since they dwell in a finitely perfect environment, they will never in fact fall into sin. Thus, it is said, the very idea of a perfect creation's going wrong spontaneously and without cause is a self-contradiction. It amounts to the self-creation of evil out of nothing! It is significant that Augustine himself, when he asks why it is that some of the angels fell while others remained steadfast, has to conclude that "These angels, therefore, either received less of the grace of the divine love than those who persevered in the same; or if both were created equally good, then, while the one fell by their evil will, the others were more abundantly assisted, and attained to the pitch of blessedness at which they have become certain that they should never fall from it."[6]

The basic criticism, then, is that a flawless creation would never go wrong and that if the creation does in fact go wrong the ultimate responsibility for this must be with its creator: for "This is where the buck stops"!

This criticism agrees with Mackie's contention (quoted on pp. 40–41) that it was logically possible for God to have created free beings who would never in fact fall. As we shall see in the next section, the alternative Irenaean theodicy takes up the further thought that although God *could* have created beings who were from the beginning finitely perfect, God has not in fact done so because such beings would never be able to become free and responsible sons and daughters of God.

A second criticism, made in the light of modern knowledge, is that we cannot today realistically think of the human species as having been once morally and spiritually perfect and then falling from that state into the chronic self-centeredness which is the human condition as we now know it. All the evidence suggests that humanity gradually emerged out of lower forms of life with a very limited moral awareness and with very crude religious conceptions. Again, it is no longer possible to regard the natural evils of disease, earthquakes, and the like as consequences of the fall of humanity, for we now know that they existed long before human beings came upon the scene. Life preyed upon life, and there were storms and earthquakes as well as disease (signs of arthritis have been found in the bones of some prehistoric animals) during the hundreds of millions of years before *homo sapiens* emerged.

A third criticism attacks the idea of the eternal torment of hell, which is affirmed to be the fate of a large proportion of the human race. Since such punishment would never end, it could serve no constructive purpose. On the contrary, it is said, it would render impossible any solution to the problem

[6]*City of God*, Bk. 12, Chap. 9.

of evil, for it would build both the sinfulness of the damned, and the nonmoral evil of their pains and sufferings, into the permanent structure of the universe.

## THE IRENAEAN THEODICY

Even from before the time of Augustine another response to the problem of evil had already been present within the developing Christian tradition. This has its basis in the thought of the early Greek-speaking Fathers of the Church, perhaps the most important of whom was St. Irenaeus (*c.* 130–*c.* 202 A.D.). He distinguished two stages of the creation of the human race.[7] In the first stage human beings were brought into existence as intelligent animals endowed with the capacity for immense moral and spiritual development. They were not the perfect pre-fallen Adam and Eve of the Augustinian tradition, but immature creatures, at the beginning of a long process of growth. In the second stage of their creation, which is now taking place, they are gradually being transformed through their own free responses from human animals into "children of God." (Irenaeus himself described the two stages as humanity being made first in the "image" and then into the "likeness" of God—referring to Genesis 1:26).

If, going beyond Irenaeus himself, we ask why humans should have been initially created as immature and imperfect beings rather than as a race of perfect creatures, the answer centers upon the positive value of human freedom. Two mutually supporting considerations are suggested. One depends upon the intuitive judgment that a human goodness that has come about through the making of free and responsible moral choices, in situations of real difficulty and temptation, is intrinsically more valuable—perhaps even limitlessly more valuable—than a goodness that has been created readymade, without the free participation of the human agent. This intuition points to the creation of the human race, not in a state of perfection, but in a state of imperfection from which it is nevertheless possible to move through moral struggle toward eventual completed humanization.

The other consideration is that if men and women had been initially created in the direct presence of God (who is infinite in life, power, goodness, and knowledge), they would have no genuine freedom in relation to their Maker. In order to be fully personal and therefore morally free beings, they have accordingly (it is suggested) been created at a distance from God—not a spatial but an epistemic distance, a distance in the dimension of knowledge. They are formed within and as part of an autonomous universe within which God is not overwhelmingly evident but in which God may become known by the free interpretative response of faith. (For more about this conception of faith, see

[7]See Irenaeus, *Against Heresies*, Book IV, Chaps. 37 and 38.

pp. 64–67.) Thus the human situation is one of tension between the natural selfishness arising from our instinct for survival, and the calls of both morality and religion to transcend our self-centeredness. Whereas the Augustinian theology sees our perfection as lying in the distant past, in an original state long since forfeited by the primordial calamity of the fall, the Irenaean type of theology sees our perfection as lying before us in the future, at the end of a lengthy and arduous process of further creation through time.

Thus the answer of the Irenaean theodicy to the question of the origin of moral evil is that it is a necessary condition of the creation of humanity at an epistemic distance from God, in a state in which one has a genuine freedom in relation to one's Maker and can freely develop, in response to God's noncoercive presence, toward one's own fulfillment as a child of God.

We may now turn to the problem of pain and suffering. Even though the bulk of actual human pain is traceable, as a sole or part cause, to misused human freedom, there remain other sources of pain that are entirely independent of the human will—for example, bacteria, earthquake, hurricane, storm, flood, drought, and blight. In practice it is often impossible to trace a boundary between the suffering that results from human wickedness and folly and that which befalls humanity from without; both are inextricably mingled in our experience. For our present purpose, however, it is important to note that the latter category does exist and that it seems to be built into the very structure of our world. In response to it, theodicy, if it is wisely conducted, follows a negative path. It is not possible to show positively that each item of human pain serves God's purpose of good; on the other hand, it does seem possible to show that the divine purpose, as it is understood in the Irenaean theology, could not be forwarded in a world that was designed as a permanent hedonistic paradise.[8]

An essential premise of this argument concerns the nature of the divine purpose in creating the world. The skeptic's normal assumption is that humanity is to be viewed as a completed creation and that God's purpose in making the world was to provide a suitable dwelling place for this fully formed creature. Since God is good and loving, the environment that God creates for human life will naturally be as pleasant and as comfortable as possible. The problem is essentially similar to that of someone who builds a cage for a pet animal. Since our world in fact contains sources of pain, hardship, and danger of innumerable kinds, the conclusion follows that this world cannot have been created by a perfectly benevolent and all-powerful deity.[9]

According to the Irenaean theodicy, however, God's purpose was not to construct a paradise whose inhabitants would experience a maximum of

[8]From the Greek *hedone*, pleasure.

[9]This is essentially David Hume's argument in his discussion of the problem of evil in his *Dialogues*, Part XI.

pleasure and a minimum of pain. The world is seen, instead, as a place of "soul making" or person making in which free beings, grappling with the tasks and challenges of their existence in a common environment, may become "children of God" and "heirs of eternal life." Our world, with all its rough edges, is the sphere in which this second and harder stage of the creative process is taking place.

This conception of the world (whether or not set in Irenaeus's theological framework) can be supported by the method of "counterfactual hypothesis." Suppose that, contrary to fact, this world were a paradise from which all possibility of pain and suffering were excluded. The consequences would be very far-reaching. For example, no one could ever injure anyone else: the murderer's knife would turn to paper or the bullets to thin air; the bank safe, robbed of a million dollars, would miraculously become filled with another million dollars; fraud, deceit, conspiracy, and treason would somehow leave the fabric of society undamaged. No one would ever be injured by accident: the mountain climber, steeplejack, or playing child falling from a height would float unharmed to the ground; the reckless driver would never meet with disaster. There would be no need to work, since no harm could result from avoiding work; there would be no call to be concerned for others in time of need or danger, for in such a world there could be no real needs or dangers.

To make possible this continual series of individual adjustments, nature would have to work by "special providences" instead of running according to general laws that we must learn to respect on penalty of pain or death. The laws of nature would have to be extremely flexible: sometimes gravity would operate, sometimes not; sometimes an object would be hard, sometimes soft. There could be no sciences, for there would be no enduring world structure to investigate. In eliminating the problems and hardships of an objective environment with its own laws, life would become like a dream in which, delightfully but aimlessly, we would float and drift at ease.[10]

One can at least begin to imagine such a world—and it is evident that in it our present ethical concepts would have no meaning. If, for example, the notion of harming someone is an essential element in the concept of a wrong action, in a hedonistic paradise there could be no wrong actions—nor therefore any right actions in distinction from wrong. Courage and fortitude would have no point in an environment in which there is, by definition, no danger or difficulty. Generosity, kindness, the *agape* aspect of love, prudence, unselfishness, and other ethical notions that presuppose life in an objective environment could not even be formed. Consequently, such a world, however well it might promote pleasure, would be very ill adapted for the development of the moral qualities of human personality. In relation to this purpose it might well be the worst of all possible worlds!

[10]Tennyson's poem, "The Lotus-Eaters," well expresses the desire (analyzed by Freud as a wish to return to the peace of the womb) for such "dreamful ease."

It would seem, then, that an environment intended to make possible the growth in free beings of the finest characteristics of personal life must have a good deal in common with our present world. It must operate according to general and dependable laws, and it must present real dangers, difficulties, problems, obstacles, and possibilities of pain, failure, sorrow, frustration, and defeat. If it did not contain the particular trials and perils that—subtracting the considerable human contribution—our world contains, it would have to contain others instead.

To realize this fact is not by any means to be in possession of a detailed theodicy. However, it is to understand that this world, with all its "heartaches and the thousand natural shocks that flesh is heir to," an environment so manifestly not designed for the maximization of human pleasure and the minimization of human pain, may nevertheless be rather well adapted to the quite different purpose of "soul making."[11]

And so the Irenaean answer to the question, Why natural evil?, is that only a world that has this general character could constitute an effective environment for the second stage (or the beginning of the second stage) of God's creative work, whereby human animals are being gradually transformed through their own free responses into "children of God."

At this point, the Irenaean theodicy points forward in three ways to the subject of life after death, which is to be discussed in later chapters.

First, although there are many striking instances of good being triumphantly brought out of evil through a person's reaction to it, there are many other cases in which the opposite has happened. Sometimes obstacles breed strength of character, dangers evoke courage and unselfishness, and calamities produce patience and moral steadfastness. On the other hand, sometimes they lead to resentment, fear, grasping selfishness, and disintegration of character. Therefore, it would seem that any divine purpose of soul making that is at work in earthly history must continue beyond this life if it is ever to achieve more than a partial and fragmentary success.

Second, if we ask the ultimate question—whether the business of person making is worth all the toil and sorrow of human life—the answer must be in terms of a future good great enough to justify all that has happened on the way to it. Its claim is that the endless enjoyment of that fullness of life and joy, beyond our present imaginations, which is the eventual fulfillment of God's love toward us, will render manifestly worthwhile all the pain and travail of the long journey of human life, both in this world and in another world or worlds as well.

---

[11]This discussion has been confined to the problem of human suffering. The large and intractable problem of animal pain is not taken up here. For a discussion of it see, for example, Austin Farrer, *Love Almighty and Ills Unlimited* (Garden City, N.Y.: Doubleday & Company, Inc., 1961), Chap. 5; and John Hick, *Evil and the God of Love*, 2nd ed. (London: Macmillan, and New York: Harper & Row, 1977), pp. 309–17. The latter book includes a comprehensive presentation of a theodicy of the Irenaean type.

Third, not only does a theodicy of the Irenaean type require a positive doctrine of life after death but, insofar as the theodicy is to be complete, it also requires that *all* human beings shall in the end attain the ultimate heavenly state.

This Irenaean type of theodicy has been criticized from a variety of points of view. Some Christian theologians have protested against its rejection of the traditional doctrines both of the fall of humanity and of the final damnation of many. Philosophical critics have argued that, while it shows with some plausibility that a person-making world cannot be a paradise, it does not thereby justify the *actual extent* of human suffering, including such gigantic evils as the Jewish Holocaust.[12] Others, however, claim that this theodicy does succeed in showing why God's world, as a sphere involving contingency and freedom, is such that even these things must, alas, be possible—even though human history would have been much better without these conspicuous crimes and horrors. There is also unresolvable disagreement as to whether so painful a creative process, even though leading to an infinite good, can be said to be the expression of divine goodness.

## PROCESS THEODICY

Process theology is a modern development in which a number of Christian theologians have adopted as their metaphysical framework the philosophy of A. N. Whitehead (1861–1947).[13] For a number of reasons, including the fact of evil in the world, process theology holds that God cannot be unlimited in power but interacts with a universe which God has not created but is nevertheless able to influence. Although different process theologians have offered hints toward a theodicy, it is only with the publication of David Griffin's *God, Power and Evil: A Process Theodicy*[14] that a systematic version has become available. An item of contrast with the more traditional Augustinian and Irenaean theodicies will provide an apt point of departure for an account of Griffin's position. According to the main Christian tradition, God is the creator and sustainer of the entire universe *ex nihilo* (out of nothing), and God's ultimate power over the creation is accordingly unlimited. However, in order to allow for the existence and growth of free human beings, God withholds the exercise of unlimited divine power, thereby forming an autonomous creaturely realm within which God acts non-coercively, seeking the creatures' free responses. Process theology likewise

---

[12]See, for example, Edward H. Madden and Peter H. Hare, *Evil and the Concept of God* (Springfield, Ill.: Charles C Thomas, 1968), Chap. 5.

[13]See John Cobb and David Griffin, *Process Theology: An Introductory Exposition* (Philadelphia: Westminster Press, 1976).

[14]David Griffin, *God, Power and Evil: A Process Theodicy* (Philadelphia: The Westminster Press, 1976). See also Barry L. Whitney, *Evil and the Process God* (New York: Mellen Press, 1985).

holds that God acts noncoercively, by "persuasion" and "lure," but in contrast to the notion of divine self-limitation, holds that God's exercise of persuasive rather than controlling power is necessitated by the ultimate metaphysical structure of reality. God is subject to the limitations imposed by the basic laws of the universe, for God has not created the universe *ex nihilo*, thereby establishing its structure, but rather the universe is an uncreated process which includes the deity. In some passages, indeed, Whitehead seems to say that the ultimate metaphysical principles were initially established by a primordial divine decision. However, Griffin follows Charles Hartshorne, another leading process thinker, in holding that those ultimate principles are eternal necessities, not matters of divine fiat. They are laws of absolute generality, such that no alternative to them is conceivable; as such they fall outside the scope even of the divine will. Accordingly, as Griffin says, "God does not refrain from controlling the creatures simply because it is better for God to use persuasion, but because it is necessarily the case that God cannot completely control the creatures."[15]

One should add at this point a second difference from traditional Christian thought, which becomes important in relation to the final outcome of the creative process. This is that for the former, in its Irenaean form, the creatures whom God is seeking to make perfect through their own freedom, were initially created by God and thus are formed with a Godward bias to their nature. For process thought, on the other hand, their very creation came about in struggle with the primordial chaos, so that the divine purpose is only imperfectly written into their nature.

The ultimate reality, according to process theology, is creativity continually producing new unities of experience out of the manifold of the previous moment. Creativity is not, however, something additional to actuality—that is, to what actually exists at a given instant—but is the creative power within all actuality. Every actuality, or "actual entity," or "actual occasion," is a momentary event, charged with creativity. As such it exerts some degree of power. It exerts power first in the way in which it receives and organizes the data of the preceding moment. This is a power of selection, exercised in positive and negative "prehensions"[16] of the data of which it thus becomes the unique "concrescence." Thus each wave of actual occasions, constituting a new moment of the universe's life, involves an element of creativity or self-causation. An actual occasion is never completely determined by the past. It is partly so determined but partly a determiner of the future, as the present occasion is itself prehended by succeeding occasions. As part determiner of the future it is again exercising power. This dual efficacy is inseparable from

---

[15]Griffin, *God, Power, and Evil*, p. 276.

[16]"The act by which an occasion of experience absorbs data from other experiences is called a 'feeling' or a 'positive prehension'. The act of excluding data from feeling is called a 'negative prehension'." *Ibid.*, p. 283.

being actual, and so every actual occasion, as a moment of creativity, necessarily exerts some degree of power.

However, finite actualities do not exercise power because God has delegated it to them, but because to be a part of the universe *is* to exercise creativity and hence power. Indeed because to be actual is to be creative, thereby exercising some degree of power, it is impossible for even God to hold a monopoly of power. Every actual occasion is, by its very nature, partially self-creative as well as partially created by previous actual occasions which were themselves partially self-created. Thus God's power over each occasion, and in directing the stream of occasions as a whole, is necessarily limited, and the reality of evil in the world is the measure of the extent to which God's will is in fact thwarted. God continually offers the best possibility to each occasion as it creates itself, but the successive occasions are free not to conform to the divine plan. And, as Whitehead says, "So far as the conformation is incomplete, there is evil in the world."[17]

Evil is, according to process theology, of two kinds, contrasting with two kinds of good. The criteria are ultimately aesthetic rather than moral. An actual occasion is a moment of experience, and the values that experience can embody are harmony and intensity. The concrescence of a multiplicity into a new complex unity, a fresh moment of experience, may be more or less richly harmonious and more or less vivid and intense. Insofar as it fails to attain harmony it exhibits the evil of discord. This discord, says Whitehead, "is the feeling of evil in the most general sense, namely physical pain or mental evil, such as sorrow, horror, dislike."[18] Insofar as a moment of experience fails to attain the highest appropriate intensity, it exhibits the other form of evil, which is needless triviality. To some extent harmony and intensity are in conflict with one another, for a higher level of intensity is made possible by increased complexity, thus endangering harmony. So one form of evil or the other, either discord or needless triviality, is virtually inevitable within the creative process. Even more important perhaps, greater complexity, making possible greater richness of experience, also makes possible new dimensions of suffering. Thus human beings can have qualities of enjoyment beyond the capacity of lower forms of life, but they are also subject to moral and spiritual anguishes which far exceed those of the lower animals and which can even drive humans to suicide. For this reason also evil is an inherent part of the creative process.

The evolution of the universe as a whole, and of life on this planet, is due to the continual divine impetus to maximize harmony and intensity in each present occasion, at the same time creating new possibilities for yet greater harmony and intensity in the future; and this divine impetus is justified on the ground that the good that has been produced, and is yet to be produced, outweighs and renders worthwhile the evil that has been produced and that

[17] A. N. Whitehead, *Religion in the Making* (New York: Cambridge University Press, 1930), p. 51.
[18] A. N. Whitehead, *Adventures of Ideas* (New York: Cambridge University Press, 1933), p. 330.

will yet be produced. For God could have left the primal chaos undisturbed instead of forming it into an ordered universe evolving ever higher forms of actuality. God is therefore responsible for having initiated and continued the development of the finite realm from disordered chaos toward ever greater possibilities of both good and evil.

Thus this particular conception of a limited deity still requires a theodicy, a justifying of God's goodness in face of the fact of evil. As Griffin says, "God is responsible in the sense of having urged the creation forward to those states in which discordant feelings could be felt with great intensity."[19] The theodicy proposed is that the good created in the course of the world process could not have come about without the possibility and, as it has turned out, the actuality of all the evil that has been inextricably intertwined with it. God's goodness is vindicated in that the risk-taking venture in the evolution of the universe was calculated to produce, and has produced, a sufficient quality and quantity of good to outweigh all the evil that has in fact been involved or that might have been involved. For the alternative to the risk of creation was not sheer nothingness but the evil of needless triviality in the primordial chaos. This theodicy is stated by Griffin in the following passage:

[The] question as to whether God is indictable is to be answered in terms of the question as to whether the positive values that are possible in our world are valuable enough to be worth the risk of the negative experiences which have occurred, and the even greater horrors which stand before us as real possibilities for the future. Should God, for the sake of avoiding the possibility of persons such as Hitler, and horrors such as Auschwitz, have precluded the possibility of Jesus, Gautama, Socrates, Confucius, Moses, Mendelssohn, El Greco, Michelangelo, Leonardo da Vinci, Florence Nightingale, Abraham Lincoln, Mahatma Gandhi, Chief Joseph, Chief Seattle, Alfred North Whitehead, John F. Kennedy, Oliver Wendell Holmes, Sojourner Truth, Helen Keller, Louis Armstrong, Albert Einstein, Dag Hammarskjold, Reinhold Niebuhr, Carol Channing, Margaret Mead, and millions of other marvelous human beings, well known and not well known alike, who have lived on the face of this earth? In other words, should God, for the sake of avoiding "man's inhumanity to man," have avoided humanity (or some comparably complex species) altogether? Only those who could sincerely answer this question affirmatively could indict the God of process theology on the basis of the evil in the world.[20]

Further, as Griffin also emphasizes, God is directly involved in the risk of creation, for the quality of the divine experience depends in part on the quality of the creatures' experiences. God shares our human joys, but also our human as well as subhuman pains. The whole weight of earthly sorrow and agony, wickedness and stupidity, passes into the divine consciousness, together with the glory of all earthly happiness and ecstasy, saintliness and genius. God, who alone knows the total balance of good and evil, finds that the risk was

[19]Griffin, *God, Power and Evil*, p. 300.
[20]*Ibid.*, p. 309.

worth taking, and this fact should help us to accept that the evil is in fact outweighed and justified by the good. As Griffin says,

Awareness of this aspect of God as envisioned by process thought not only removes the basis for that sense of moral outrage which would be directed toward an impassive spectator deity who took great risks with the creation. It also provides an additional basis, beyond that of our own immediate experience, for affirming that the risk was worth taking. That being who is the universal agent, goading the creation to overcome triviality in favour of the more intense harmonies, is also the universal recipient of the totality of good and evil that is actualized. In other words, the one being who is in a position to know experientially the bitter as well as the sweet fruits of the risk of creation is the same being who has encouraged and continues to encourage this process of creative risk taking.[21]

Such a theodicy appeals in two main ways. One is that it avoids the traditional problem arising from the belief in divine omnipotence. God is not the all-powerful creator of the universe, responsible for its character, but is a part—though a uniquely basic part—of the universe itself, unable either to vary its fundamental structure or to intervene directly in its changing details. Thus God does not need to be justified for permitting evil, since it is not within God's power to prevent it. (This point is however qualified in Griffin's presentation; according to him, God could have refrained from "luring" the universe on in the evolutionary development which has produced animal and human life, with all its pain and suffering.) The other appeal consists in the stirring summons to engage on God's side in the never-ending struggle against the evils of an intractable world. This was the moral appeal of earlier forms of belief in a finite God who claims our support in the ongoing battle of light against darkness—as in ancient Zoroastrianism and Manichaeism, or (as a tentative hypothesis) in the thought of John Stuart Mill, who wrote:

A creed like this…allows it to be believed that all the mass of evil which exists was undesigned by, and exists not by the appointment of, but in spite of the Being whom we are called upon to worship. A virtuous human being assumes in this theory the exalted character of a fellow-labourer with the Highest, a fellow combatant in the great strife….[22]

However, despite its appeal, the process theodicy has been severely criticized.[23]

One basic claim—with which process theologians would not, needless to say, agree—is that it involves a morally and religiously unacceptable elitism. In all ages the majority of people have lived in hunger or the threat and fear of hunger—often severely undernourished, subject to crippling injuries and

---

[21]*Ibid.*, pp. 309–10.

[22]John Stuart Mill, *Three Essays on Religion* (London: Longmans, 1875, and Westport, Conn.: Greenwood Press), pp. 116–17.

[23]See, for example, Madden and Hare, *Evil and the Concept of God*, Chap. 6.

debilitating diseases, so that only the fittest could survive infancy—and they have dwelt under conditions of oppression or slavery and in a constant state of insecurity and anxiety. As Barbara Ward and René Dubos put it in their survey of the human condition:

The actual life of most of mankind has been cramped with back-breaking labour, exposed to deadly or debilitating diseases, prey to wars and famines, haunted by the loss of children, filled with fear and the ignorance that breeds more fear. At the end, for everyone, stands dreaded unknown death. To long for joy, support and comfort, to react violently against fear and anguish is quite simply the human condition.[24]

The process theodicy does not suggest that it is their own individual fault that hundreds of millions of human beings have been born into and have had to endure this situation. The high intensity of physical and mental suffering that is possible at the human level of experience is just part of the actual process of the universe. It seems to be entailed by Griffin's process theodicy that what makes all this acceptable to God is the fact that the same complex process which has produced all this suffering has also produced the cream of the human species. But for each one such "marvelous human being," perhaps tens of thousands of others have existed without any significant degree of personal freedom and without any opportunity for intellectual, moral, aesthetic, or spiritual development; their lives have been spent in a desperate and often degrading struggle to survive. We have already noted that, according to process theology, the whole weight of earthly sorrow and agony passes into the divine consciousness; in Whitehead's words, God is "the fellow sufferer who understands."[25] But nevertheless, God is apparently content that this great mass of human suffering has been endured and this great mass of human potentiality has been undeveloped because, as part of the same world process, the elite have fulfilled in themselves some of the finer possibilities of human existence.

It would of course be quite wrong to say that, within the process theodicy, the unfortunate have suffered deprivation *in order that* the fortunate may enjoy their blessings. It is not that some have been deliberately sacrificed for the good of others. The more extreme evils of human cruelty and neglect, injustice and exploitation, might conceivably never have occurred—and the creative process would have been the better without them. The process doctrine (as presented by Griffin) is rather that the possibility of creating the degree of human good that has in fact come about involved the possibility of creating also the degree of human evil that has in fact come about. According to this theodicy, the good that has occurred renders worthwhile all the wickedness that has been committed and all the suffering that has been endured.

[24]Barbara Ward and René Dubos, *Only One Earth* (New York: W. W. Norton & Co., Inc., 1972), p.35.

[25]Alfred Whitehead, *Process and Reality* (Cambridge: Oxford University Press, 1929), p. 497.

Clearly, it can be questioned whether such a God is to be equated with the God of the New Testament, understood as the Creator who values all human creatures with a universal and impartial love. Clearly, again, this is far from being the God of contemporary liberation theology, who is the God of the poor and the oppressed, the enslaved and all against whom the structures of human society discriminate.[26] These individuals are deprived of the opportunity of developing the moral and spiritual, intellectual and aesthetic potentialities of their nature. The God of the process theodicy is—according to this line of criticism—the God of the elite, of the great and successful among humankind. God is apparently the God of saints rather than of sinners; of geniuses rather than of the dull, retarded, and mentally defective; of the cream of humanity rather than of the anonymous millions who have been driven to self-seeking, violence, greed, and deceit in a desperate struggle to survive. This is not the God of those millions who have been crippled by malnutrition and have suffered and died under oppression and exploitation, plague and famine, flood and earthquake, or again of those—perhaps numbering about half the sum of human births—who have perished in infancy.

For the God of this form of process theodicy, although not the ultimate maker and lord of the universe (for there is no such), is still responsible for having elicited human existence out of the earlier stages of life, risking the vast dead-weight of human suffering and the virulent power of human wicked- ness, for the sake of the morally and spiritually successful in whom God rejoices. God may indeed, as Griffin suggests, find the total spectacle of human life through the ages to be good on balance; for in the total divine experience the sufferings of those who suffer, and the inadequacies of those whose human potential remains undeveloped, are overbalanced by the happiness and achievements of the fortunate. However, the starving and the oppressed, the victims of Auschwitz, the human wrecks who are irreparably brain-damaged or mind-damaged, and those others who have loved and agonized over them, can hardly be expected to share the process God's point of view or to regard such a God as worthy of their worship and praise. It is not they but others who benefit from the bracing doctrine, reminiscent of nineteenth-century *laissez- faire* capitalist theory, that though the weak may go to the wall, the system as a whole is good because it also produces those who are spiritually and culturally rich.

The situation would, of course, be transformed if a process theodicy were able to affirm the eventual successful completion of the creative process in a future heavenly fulfillment in which all are eventually to participate. Then the tragedy of human life, though real, would not be ultimate; it would be woven

---

[26]This charge seems to me to hold despite the fact that some of the process theologians have aligned themselves with the contemporary liberation theology movement. (See Schubert Ogden, *Faith and Freedom: Toward a Theology of Liberation*, Nashville: Abingdon, 1979, and John B. Cobb, Jr., *Process Theology as Political Theology*, Philadelphia: Westminster Press, 1982.) For the question remains whether this move is compatible with the process theodicy presented by Griffin.

into what Dante called the Divine Comedy of God's total creative action. Then it would be true that, in Mother Julian's phrase, "all shall be well, and all shall be well, and all manner of thing shall be well." However, Griffin, while not excluding the possibility of continued human existence after death in a disembodied state, is emphatic that we cannot draw from this possibility the hope of a limitless final good to justify all the evil that will have occurred on the way to it. He is insistent that any justification must be found in the actual character of human existence in this world. He can even contemplate the possibility of a nuclear or environmental disaster which annihilates the human race, or which reduces the survivors to a state of brutality and misery, and can say that "No matter how bad the future actually turns out to be, it will not cancel out the worthwhileness of the human goodness enjoyed during the previous thousands of years."[27]

In suggesting that Griffin's process theodicy is elitist in a way that violates the basic Christian conviction of God's love for all human creatures, one is perhaps complaining that its ultimate principle is aesthetic rather than ethical. To some, such an approach seems appropriate, while to others, it is not.

Returning now to the problem of evil as a challenge to theistic belief, we can see that there are various ways in which the challenge has been sought to be met. One or other of these ways has seemed sufficient to many religious believers—sufficient, that is, to show that intellectually there is no need to abandon belief in God, even though of course no amount of intellectual justification can hope to assuage the actual pains and sorrows and sufferings of the human heart.

[27]Griffin, *God, Power and Evil*, p. 313.

# CHAPTER 5

# Revelation and Faith

---

It seems, then, that the universe is religiously ambiguous—capable of being construed both religiously and naturalistically. This is tacitly acknowledged by the traditional term used for human awareness of God, namely faith, as distinguished from knowledge. It is therefore to the concept of faith, and the correlative concept of revelation, that we now turn.

## THE PROPOSITIONAL VIEW OF REVELATION AND FAITH

Christian thought contains two very different understandings of the nature of revelation and, as a result, two different conceptions of faith (as the human reception of revelation), of the Bible (as a medium of revelation), and of theology (as discourse based upon revelation).

The view that dominates the medieval period and that is represented today by more traditional forms of Roman Catholicism (and also, in a curious meeting of opposites, by conservative Protestantism) can be called the "propositional" understanding of revelation. According to this view, the content of revelation is a body of truths expressed in statements or propositions. Revelation is the imparting to people of divinely authenticated truths. In the words of the older *Catholic Encyclopedia*, "Revelation may be defined as the communication of some truth by God to a rational creature through means which are beyond the ordinary course of nature."[1]

---

[1] *The Catholic Encyclopedia* (New York: Robert Appleton Co., 1912), XIII, 1.

Corresponding to this conception of revelation is a view of faith as people's obedient acceptance of these divinely revealed truths. Thus faith was defined by the Vatican Council of 1870 as "a supernatural virtue whereby, inspired and assisted by the grace of God, we believe that the things that He has revealed are true." Or again, a recent American Jesuit theologian writes, "To a Catholic, the word 'faith' conveys the notion of an intellectual assent to the content of revelation as true because of the witnessing authority of God the Revealer...Faith is the Catholic's response to an intellectual message communicated by God."[2]

These two interdependent conceptions of revelation as the divine promulgation of religious truths, and of faith as our obedient reception of these truths, are related to a view of the Bible as the place where those truths are authoritatively written down. They were first revealed through the prophets, then more fully and perfectly through Christ and the apostles, and are now recorded in the Scriptures. It is thus an essential element of this view that the Bible is not a merely human, and therefore fallible, book. The First Vatican Council formulated Roman Catholic belief for the modern period by saying of the books of the Bible that "...having been written by inspiration of the Holy Ghost, they have God for their author." (One may compare with this the words of the Protestant evangelist, Dr. Billy Graham, "The Bible is a book written by God through thirty secretaries.") It should be added, however, that in Catholic theology Scripture is set within the context of tradition. Thus, the Council of Trent (1546–1563) declared that "...with the same devotion and reverence with which it accepts and venerates all the books of the Old and New Testament, since one God is the author of both, it also accepts and venerates traditions concerned with faith and morals as having been received orally from Christ or inspired by the Holy Spirit and continuously preserved in the Catholic Church." Protestantism, on the other hand, recognizes no such oral tradition possessing equal authority with the Bible and claims that through the Bible God speaks directly to the Church as a whole and to the mind and conscience of individual believers.

This same propositional conception of revelation as God's imparting of certain truths that have been inscribed in the sacred Scriptures, and are believed by faith, leads also to a particular view of the nature and function of theology. The propositional theory of revelation has always been accompanied by the distinction between natural and revealed theology. This distinction has been almost universally accepted by Christian theologians of all traditions until the present century. Natural theology was held to consist of all those theological truths that can be worked out by the unaided human

[2]Gustave Weigel, *Faith and Understanding in America* (New York: The Macmillan Company, 1959), p. 1. On the other hand, in more recent Catholic writings there is a growing tendency to recognize other aspects of faith in addition to the element of intellectual assent. See Karl Rahner, ed., *Encyclopedia of Theology* (London: Burns & Oates and New York: Crossroad Publishing Company, 1975).

intellect. It was believed, for example, that the existence and attributes of God and the immortality of the soul can be proved by strict logical argument involving no appeal to revelation. Revealed theology, on the other hand, was held to consist of those further truths that are not accessible to human reason and that can be known to us only if they are specially revealed by God. For example, it was held that although the human mind, by right reasoning, can attain the truth that God exists, it cannot arrive in the same way at the further truth that God is three Persons in one; thus the doctrine of the Trinity was considered to be an item of revealed theology, to be accepted by faith. (The truths of natural theology were believed to have been also revealed, for the benefit of those who lack the time or the mental equipment to arrive at them for themselves.)

Many modern philosophical treatments of religion, whether attacking or defending it, presuppose this propositional view of revelation and faith. For example, Walter Kaufmann, in his lively and provocative *Critique of Religion and Philosophy*, assumed that the religious person who appeals to revelation is referring to theological propositions that God is supposed to have declared to humankind.[3] Indeed, probably the majority of recent philosophical critics of religion have had in mind a definition of faith as the believing of propositions upon insufficient evidence.[4]

Many philosophical defenders of religion share the same assumption and propose various expedients to compensate for the lack of evidence to support their basic convictions. The most popular way of bridging the evidential gap is by an effort of the will. Thus, one recent religious philosopher stated that "…faith is distinguished from the entertainment of a probable proposition by the fact that the latter can be a completely theoretic affair. Faith is a 'yes' of self-commitment, it does not turn probabilities into certainties; only a sufficient increase in the weight of evidence could do that. But it is a volitional response which takes us out of the theoretic attitude."[5]

This emphasis upon the part played by the will in religious faith (an emphasis that goes back at least as far as Aquinas[6]) has provided the basis for a number of modern theories of the nature of faith, some of which will now be discussed.

[3]Walter Kaufmann, *Critique of Religion and Philosophy* (New York: Harper & Row, Publishers, 1958). For example, "Even if we grant, for the sake of the present argument, that God exists and sometimes reveals propositions to mankind…" (p. 89).

[4]For example, "The general sense is belief, perhaps based on some evidence, but very firm, or at least more firm, or/and of more extensive content, than the evidence possessed by the believer rationally warrants." C. J. Ducasse, *A Philosophical Scrutiny of Religion* (New York: The Ronald Press Company, 1953), pp. 73–74. Copyright 1953 by The Ronald Press.

[5]Dorothy Emmet, *The Nature of Metaphysical Thinking* (London: Macmillan & Company Ltd., 1945), p. 140.

[6]*Summa Theologica*, Second Part of the Second Part, Question 2, Art. 9.

## VOLUNTARIST THEORIES OF FAITH

The classic treatments of religious faith as the acceptance of certain beliefs by a deliberate act of will are those of the seventeenth-century French thinker Blaise Pascal and the nineteenth-century American philosopher and psychologist William James.

Pascal's "Wager" treats the question of divine existence as an enigma concerning which we can take up a position only on the basis of a calculation of risks. If we wager our lives that God exists, we stand to gain eternal salvation if we are right and to lose little if we are wrong. If, on the other hand, we wager our lives that there is no God, we stand to gain little if we are right but to lose eternal happiness if we are wrong. "Let us weigh the gain and the loss in wagering that God is. Let us estimate these two chances. If you gain, you gain all; if you lose, you lose nothing. Wager, then, without hesitation that He is."[7]

If we ask whether it is possible to make oneself believe in God, Pascal answers that this *is* possible—not indeed instantaneously, but by a course of treatment. "You would like to attain faith, and do not know the way; you would like to cure yourself of unbelief, and ask the remedy for it. Learn of those who have been bound like you....Follow the way by which they began; by acting as if they believed, taking the holy water, having masses said, etc. Even this will naturally make you believe, and deaden your acuteness."[8]

Given an anthropomorphic (and to many people, very unattractive) conception of God, Pascal's Wager amounts to a rational form of self-insurance. It assumes that God will be pleased by such a calculating and self-regarding attitude. The assumption has seemed profoundly irreligious to many religious believers, although it has also been seriously adopted by others.[9]

William James (1842–1910), a founder of the pragmatist school of thought, argues in his famous essay "The Will to Believe" (1897) that the existence or nonexistence of God, of which there can be no conclusive evidence either way, is a matter of such momentous importance that anyone who so desires has the right to stake one's life upon the God hypothesis. Indeed, we are obliged to bet our lives upon either this or the contrary possibility. "We cannot escape the issue by remaining skeptical and waiting for more light, because, although we do avoid error in that way *if religion be untrue*, we lose the good, *if it be true*, just as certainly as if we positively chose to disbelieve." James continues:

---

[7]Pascal, *Pensées*, trans. F. W. Trotter (London: J. M. Dent & Sons Ltd. and New York: E. P. Dutton & Co., Inc., 1932), No. 233, p. 67.

[8]*Ibid.*, p. 68.

[9]Pascal's Wager is used as an apologetic device by, for example, Edward J. Carnell, *An Introduction to Christian Apologetics* (Grand Rapids, Mich.: W. B. Eerdmans Publishing Co., 1948), pp. 357–59.

*Better risk loss of truth than chance of error*—that is your faith-vetoer's exact position. He is actively playing his stake as much as the believer is; he is backing the field against the religious hypothesis, just as the believer is backing the religious hypothesis against the field. To preach scepticism to us as a duty until "sufficient evidence" for religion be found, is tantamount therefore to telling us, when in presence of the religious hypothesis, that to yield to our fear of its being error is wiser and better than to yield to our hope that it may be true....Dupery for dupery, what proof is there that dupery through hope is so much worse than dupery through fear? I, for one, can see no proof; and I simply refuse obedience to the scientist's command to imitate his kind of option, in a case where my own stake is important enough to give me the right to choose my own form of risk.[10]

Further, if there is a personal God, our unwillingness to proceed on the supposition that he is real may make it impossible for us ever to be accepted by him: "…just as a man who in a company of gentlemen made no advances, asked a warrant for every concession, and believed no one's word without proof, would cut himself off by such churlishness from all the social rewards that a more trustworthy spirit would earn—so here, one who would shut himself up in snarling logicality and try to make the gods extort his recognition willy-nilly, or not get it at all, might cut himself off forever from his only opportunity of making the gods' acquaintance."[11]

The basic weakness of James's position is that it constitutes an unrestricted license for wishful thinking. James, at one point, imagines the Mahdi to write to us saying, "I am the Expected One whom God has created in his effulgence. You shall be infinitely happy if you confess me; otherwise you shall be cut off from the light of the sun. Weigh, then, your infinite gain if I am genuine against your finite sacrifice if I am not!"[12] The only reason that James could offer for not responding to this pressing invitation is that it did not rank as a "live option" in his mind. That is to say, it did not conform to the assumptions presently controlling his thinking. However, the fact that it was not a live option for James is an accidental circumstance that cannot affect the truth or falsity of the Mahdi's assertions. An idea might be true, although it did not presently appeal to William James; but if the idea were true, James would never come to know it by his method, a method that could result only in everyone's becoming more firmly entrenched in his or her current prejudices. A procedure having this effect can hardly claim to be designed for the discovery of truth. It amounts to an encouragement to us all to believe, at our own risk, whatever we like. However, if our aim is to believe what is *true*, and not necessarily what we *like*, James's universal permissiveness will not help us.[13]

---

[10]William James in *The Will to Believe and Other Essays* (New York: Longmans, Green & Co., Inc., 1897), pp. 26–27.

[11]*Ibid.*, p. 28.

[12]James, *The Will to Believe*, p. 7.

[13]For a more sympathetic response to James, see, for example, Stephen T. Davis, *Faith, Skepticism and Evidence* (Lewisburg: Bucknell University Press, 1978), Part II.

Another philosophical theologian, F. R. Tennant, identified faith with the element of willing venture in all discovery. He distinguished faith from belief as follows:

Belief is more or less constrained by fact or Actuality that already is or will be, independently of any striving of ours, and which convinces us. Faith, on the other hand, reaches beyond the Actual or the given to the ideally possible, which in the first instance it creates, as the mathematician posits his entities, and then by practical activity may realize or bring into Actuality. Every machine of human invention has thus come to be. Again, faith may similarly lead to knowledge of Actuality which it in no sense creates, but which would have continued, in absence of the faith-venture, to be unknown: as in the discovery of America by Columbus.[14]

Tennant freely allowed that there can be no general guarantee that faith will be justified. "Hopeful experimenting has not produced the machine capable of perpetual motion; and had Columbus steered with confidence for Utopia, he would not have found it."[15] Faith always involves risks; but it is only by such risks that human knowledge is extended. Science and religion are alike in requiring the venture of faith. "Science postulates what is requisite to make the world amenable to the kind of thought that conceives of the structure of the universe, and its orderedness according to quantitative law; theology, and sciences of valuation, postulate what is requisite to make the world amenable to the kind of thought that conceives of the why and wherefore, the meaning or purpose of the universe, and its orderedness according to teleological principles."[16]

Tennant's bracketing together of religious faith and scientific "faith" is highly questionable. A scientist's "faith" is significant only as a preliminary to experimental testing. It is often a necessary stage on the way to tested knowledge, and it has value only in relation to subsequent verification. In science, verification "...consists in finding that the postulate or theory is borne out by appeal to external facts and tallies with them."[17] But religious faith, according to Tennant, can hope for no such objective verification. It consists in the inwardly satisfying and spiritually fortifying effects of faith upon the believer. "Successful faith...is illustrated by numerous examples of the gaining of material and moral advantages, the surmounting of trials and afflictions, and the attainment of heroic life, by men of old who were inspired by faith. It is thus that faith is pragmatically 'verified' and that certitude as to the unseen is established." However, even this purely subjective verification is undermined by the inevitable concession that "...such verification is only for

---

[14]F. R. Tennant, *Philosophical Theology* (Cambridge: Cambridge University Press, 1928), I, 297. Tennant also expounded his theory in *The Nature of Belief* (London: The Centenary Press, 1943).

[15]*Ibid.*

[16]*Ibid.*, p. 299.

[17]Tennant, *The Nature of Belief*, p. 70.

[subjective] certitude, not a proving of [objective] certainty as to external reality. The fruitfulness of a belief or of faith for the moral and religious life is one thing, and the reality or existence of what is ideated and assumed is another. There are instances in which a belief that is not true, in the sense of corresponding with fact, may inspire one with lofty ideals and stimulate one to strive to be a more worthy person."[18] This admission reduces religious faith, as Tennant conceives it, to an unverifiable hope, and thereby undermines his attempt to assimilate religious to scientific cognition.

## TILLICH'S CONCEPTION OF FAITH AS ULTIMATE CONCERN

Another conception of faith, differing from those so far mentioned, is that of Paul Tillich, who taught that "Faith is the state of being ultimately concerned."[19] Our ultimate concern is that which determines our being or nonbeing—not in the sense of our physical existence but in the sense of "...the reality, the structure, the meaning, and the aim of existence."[20] People are, in fact, ultimately concerned about many different things—for example, their nation, or their personal success and status; but these are properly only preliminary concerns, and the elevation of preliminary concern to ultimacy is idolatry. Tillich describes ultimate concern in an often-quoted passage:

Ultimate concern is the abstract translation of the great commandment: "The Lord, our God, the Lord is one; and you shall love the Lord your God with all your heart, and with all your soul, and with all your mind, and with all your strength." The religious concern is ultimate; it excludes all other concerns from ultimate significance; it makes them preliminary. The ultimate concern is unconditional, independent of any conditions of character, desire, or circumstance. The unconditional concern is total: no part of ourselves or of our world is excluded from it; there is no "place" to flee from it. The total concern is infinite: no moment of relaxation and rest is possible in the face of a religious concern which is ultimate, unconditional, total, and infinite.[21]

This passage well exhibits the ambiguity of the phrase "ultimate concern," which may refer either to an *attitude* of concern or to the (real or imagined) *object* of that attitude. Does "ultimate concern" refer to a concerned state of mind or to a supposed object of this state of mind? Of the four adjectives that Tillich uses in this passage, "unconditional" suggests that it refers to an attitude of concern, "infinite" suggests that it refers to an object of concern, and "ultimate" and "total" could perhaps apply to either. From the pages of

[18]*Ibid.*

[19]Paul Tillich, *Dynamics of Faith* (New York: Harper & Row, Publishers, 1957), p. 1.

[20]Paul Tillich, *Systematic Theology* (Chicago: Chicago University Press, 1951), I, 14. Copyright 1951 by the University of Chicago.

[21]*Ibid.*, pp. 11–12.

his *Systematic Theology*, it is indeed impossible to tell which meaning Tillich intends or whether he has in mind both at once or sometimes one and sometimes the other.

In his later book, *Dynamics of Faith*, this ambiguity is resolved. Tillich explicitly adopts both of these two possible meanings by identifying the attitude of ultimate concern with the object of ultimate concern. "The ultimate of the act of faith and the ultimate that is meant in the act of faith are one and the same." This means the "…disappearance of the ordinary subject–object scheme in the experience of the ultimate, the unconditional."[22] That is to say, ultimate concern is not a matter of the human subject adopting a certain attitude to a divine Object but is, in Tillichian language, a form of the human mind's participation in the Ground of its own being. This notion of participation is fundamental to Tillich's thought. He contrasts two types of philosophy of religion, which he describes as ontological and cosmological.[23] The latter (which he associates with Aquinas) thinks of God as being "out there," to be reached only at the end of a long and hazardous process of inference; to find him is to meet a Stranger. For the ontological approach, which Tillich espouses and which he associates with Augustine, God is already present to us as the Ground of our own being, and yet at the same time infinitely transcends us. Our finite being is continuous with the infinity of Being; consequently, to know God means to overcome our estrangement from the Ground of our being. God is not Another, an Object which we may know or fail to know, but Being-itself, in which we participate by the very fact of existing. To be ultimately concerned about God is to express our true relationship to Being.

As in the case of other elements in his system, Tillich's definition of faith as ultimate concern is capable of being developed in different directions. Stressing the removal of the subject–object dichotomy, his definition of faith can be seen as pointing to humanity's continuity or even identity with God as the Ground of being. But it can also be seen as pointing in the opposite direction, toward so extreme a sundering of God and man that faith can operate as an autonomous function of the mind whether God be a reality or not. Tillich presents this view in the following passage:

"God"…is the name for that which concerns man ultimately. This does not mean that first there is a being called God and then the demand that man should be ultimately concerned about him. It means that whatever concerns a man ultimately becomes god for him, and, conversely, it means that a man can be concerned ultimately only about that which is god for him.[24]

[22]Tillich, *Dynamics of Faith*, p. 11.

[23]"The Two Types of Philosophy of Religion," *Theology of Culture* (New York: Oxford University Press, Inc., 1959). Reprinted in John Hick, ed., *Classical and Contemporary Readings in the Philosophy of Religion*, 3rd ed. (Englewood Cliffs, N.J.: Prentice-Hall, Inc., 1989).

[24]Tillich, *Systematic Theology*, I, 211.

Thus, with Tillich's formula, one can either define faith in terms of God, as one's concern about the Ultimate, or define God in terms of faith, as that—whatever it may be—about which one is ultimately concerned. This permissiveness between supranaturalism and naturalism is regarded by Tillich as constituting a third and superior standpoint "beyond naturalism and supranaturalism."[25] Whether Tillich is justified in regarding it in this way is a question for readers to consider for themselves.

## A NONPROPOSITIONAL VIEW OF REVELATION AND FAITH

A different view of revelation, which can be called in contrast the "nonpropositional" view (or, if a technical term is desired, the *heilsgeschichtliche* view), has become widespread within Protestant Christianity during the present century. This view claims to have its roots in the thought of the Reformers of the sixteenth century (Luther and Calvin and their associates) and still further back in the New Testament and the early Church.[26]

According to this nonpropositional view, the content of revelation is not a body of truths about God, but God coming within the orbit of human experience by acting in history. From this point of view, theological propositions, as such, are not revealed but represent human attempts to understand the significance of revelatory events. This nonpropositional conception of revelation is connected with the modern renewed emphasis upon the *personal* character of God and the thought that the divine–human personal relationship consists of something more than the promulgation and reception of theological truths. Certain questions at once present themselves.

If it is God's intention to confront us with God's presence, as personal will and purpose, why has this not been done in an unambiguous manner, by some overwhelming manifestation of divine power and glory?

The answer that is generally given runs parallel to one of the considerations that occurred in connection with the problem of evil. If one is to have the freedom necessary for a relationship of love and trust, this freedom must extend to the basic and all-important matter of one's consciousness of God. God (as conceived in the Judaic-Christian tradition) is such that to be aware of God is, in important respects, unlike being aware of a finite person. The existence of a fellow human being can be a matter of indifference to us. The obvious exception is that consciousness of another which is love. The peculiarly self-involving awareness of love thus bears a certain analogy to our awareness of God. In love, the existence of the beloved, far from being a matter

---

[25]*Ibid.*, 5f.

[26]For an account of the development from the propositional to the nonpropositional view in modern Protestant thought, see John Baillie, *The Idea of Revelation in Recent Thought* (New York: Columbia University Press, 1956).

of indifference, affects one's whole being. God, the object of the religious consciousness, is such that it is impossible for a finite creature to be aware of God and yet remain unaffected by this awareness. God, according to the Judaic-Christian tradition, is the source and ground of our being. It is by God's will that we exist. God's purpose for us is so indelibly written into our nature that the fulfillment of this purpose is the basic condition of our own personal self-fulfillment and happiness. We are thus totally dependent upon God as the giver not only of our existence but also of our highest good. To become conscious of God is to see oneself as a created, dependent creature receiving life and well-being from a higher source. In relation to this higher Being, self-disclosed to us as holy love, the only appropriate attitude is one of grateful worship and obedience. Thus, the process of becoming aware of God, if it is not to destroy the frail autonomy of the human personality, must involve the individual's own freely responding insight and assent. Therefore, it is said, God does not become known to us as a reality of the same order as ourselves, for then the finite being would be swallowed by the infinite Being. Instead, God has created space-time as a sphere in which we may exist in relative independence, as spatiotemporal creatures. Within this sphere God is self-discovered in ways that allow us the fateful freedom to recognize or fail to recognize God's presence. Divine activity always leaves room for that uncompelled response that theology calls faith. It is this element in the awareness of God that preserves our human cognitive freedom in relation to an infinitely greater and superior reality. Faith is thus the correlate of freedom: faith is related to cognition as free will to conation. As one of the early Church Fathers wrote, "And not merely in works, but also in faith, has God preserved the will of man free and under his own control."[27]

In ordinary nonreligious experience, there is something epistemologically similar to this in the phenomenon of "seeing as," which was brought to the attention of philosophers by Ludwig Wittgenstein (1889–1951) when he pointed out the epistemological interest of puzzle pictures.[28] Consider, for example, the page covered with apparently random dots and lines, which, as one gazes at it, suddenly takes the form of a picture of (say) human beings standing in a grove of trees. The entire field of dots and lines is now seen as having this particular kind of significance and no longer as merely a haphazard array of marks.

We can develop this idea and suggest that in addition to such purely visual interpreting, there is also the more complex phenomenon of *experiencing as*, in which a whole situation is experienced as having some specific significance. A familiar example of a situation that is perceived with all the senses and has

[27]Irenaeus, *Against Heresies*, Book IV, Chap. 37, para. 5.
[28]Ludwig Wittgenstein, *Philosophical Investigations* (Oxford: Basil Blackwell and New York: Mott Ltd., 1953), Part II, Sec. xi.

its own practical significance is that of driving an automobile along a highway. To be conscious of being in this particular kind of situation is to be aware that certain reactions (and dispositions to react) are appropriate and others inappropriate; an important part of our consciousness of the situation as having the character that it has consists in our readiness to act appropriately within it. Anyone would react in characteristically different ways in the midst of a battle and on a quiet Sunday afternoon stroll; a person would do so in recognition of the differing characters of these two types of situation. Such awareness is a matter of "experiencing as." The significance of a given situation for a given observer consists primarily of its bearing upon that person's behavioral dispositions. Being an interpretative act, "experiencing as" can of course be mistaken, as—to mention an extreme case—when a mentally-ill person feels that everyone poses a threat, and reacts accordingly.

Sometimes two different orders or levels of significance are experienced within the same situation; this is what happens when the religious mind experiences events both as occurring within human history and also as mediating the presence and activity of God. A religious significance is found superimposed upon the natural significance of the situation in the believer's experience.

Thus, for example, the ancient Hebrew prophets saw the events of their contemporary history both as interactions between Israel and the surrounding nations and, at the same time, as God's dealings with the people of Israel— leading, guiding, disciplining, and punishing them in order that they might be instruments of God's purpose. In the prophetic interpretation of history embodied in the Hebrew scriptures, events that would be described by a secular historian as the outcome of political, economic, sociological, and geographical factors are seen as incidents in a dialogue that continues through the centuries between God and Israel. It is important to realize that the prophets were not formulating a philosophy of history in the sense of a hypothesis applied retrospectively to the facts; instead, they were reporting their actual experience of the events as they happened. They were conscious of living in the midst of *Heilsgeschichte*, salvation–history. They saw God actively at work in the world around them. For example, a classic commentary says of the time when the Chaldean army was attacking Jerusalem, "Behind the serried ranks of the Chaldean army [Jeremiah] beheld the form of Jahweh fighting for them and through them against His own people."[29] The prophets experienced their contemporary situations as moments in which God was actively present.

The same epistemological pattern—the interpreting in a distinctive way of events that are in themselves capable of being construed either naturalistically or religiously—runs through the New Testament. Here again, in the story of a man, Jesus of Nazareth, and a movement which arose in connection with

---

[29]John Skinner, *Prophecy and Religion* (Cambridge: Cambridge University Press, 1922), p. 261.

him, there are ambiguous data. It is possible to see him simply as a self-appointed prophet who got mixed up in politics, clashed with the Jerusalem priesthood, and had to be eliminated. It is also possible, with the New Testament writers, to see him as the Messiah of God giving himself for the renewing of humankind. To see him in this way is to share the faith or the distinctive way of "experiencing as" which gave rise to the New Testament documents.[30]

This theme of God as *deus absconditus*, the hidden God, who comes to men in the incognito of a human life in order to preserve people's freedom, is found in Martin Luther and is expressed with great clarity by Pascal:

It was not then right that He should appear in a manner manifestly divine, and completely capable of convincing all men; but it was also not right that He should come in so hidden a manner that He could not be known by those who should sincerely seek Him. He has willed to make Himself quite recognizable by those; and thus, willing to appear openly to those who seek Him with all their heart, and to be hidden from those who flee from Him with all their heart, He so regulates the knowledge of Himself that He has given signs of Himself, visible to those who seek Him, and not to those who seek Him not. There is enough light for those who only desire to see, and enough obscurity for those who have a contrary disposition.[31]

More broadly, religious apperception, within the Judaic-Christian tradition, experiences human life as a situation in which people are at all times having to do with God and God with them. The ethic that is an inseparable aspect of this faith indicates the way in which it is appropriate to behave in such a situation.

---

[30]This view of the nature of religious faith is presented more fully in John Hick, *Faith and Knowledge*, 2nd ed., 1966, (Reissued, London: Macmillan, 1988), Chaps. 5–6. This and many other topics in the epistemology of religion are illuminatingly discussed in Terence Penelhum, *Problems of Religious Knowledge* (London: Macmillan & Company Ltd. and New York: Herder & Herder, Inc., 1971).

[31]*Pensées*, trans. W. F. Trotter (London: J. M. Dent & Sons Ltd. and New York: E. P. Dutton & Co., Inc., 1932), No. 430, p. 118.

# CHAPTER 6

# Evidentialism, Foundationalism, and Rational Belief

## THE LIMITS OF PROOF

We return now to our central question concerning the Judaic-Christian concept of God: What grounds are there for believing that any such being exists?

We saw in Chapters 2, 3, and 4 that it is not possible to establish either the existence or the nonexistence of God by rational arguments proceeding from universally accepted premises. We saw also that arguments to the effect that theism is more probable than naturalism, or naturalism than theism, are basically defective, since the term "probable" lacks a precise meaning in this context.

In spite of the immense intellectual investment that has gone into the various attempts to demonstrate the existence of God, the conclusion that this is indemonstrable agrees not only with the contemporary philosophical understanding of the nature and limits of logical proof but also with the biblical understanding of our knowledge of God.

Philosophy recognizes two ways in which human beings may come to know whatever there is to be known. One way (stressed by empiricism) is through experience, and the other (stressed by rationalism) is through reasoning. The limitation of the rationalist way is that the only truths capable of being strictly proved are analytic and ultimately tautological. We cannot by logic alone demonstrate any matters of fact and existence; these must be known through experience. That two and two equal four can be certified by strict proof; but that we live in a world of objects in space, and that there is this table and that oak tree and those people, are facts that could never be known independently of sense perception. If nothing were given through experience in its various modes, we should never have anything to reason about. This is as true in religion as in other fields. If God exists, God is not an idea but a reality outside us; in order to be known to men and women, God must therefore become manifest in some way within their experience.

This conclusion is in line with the contemporary revolt against the rationalist assumptions which have dominated much of western philosophy since the time of Descartes. Descartes held that we can properly be said to know only truths that are self-evident or that can be reached by logical inferences from self-evident premises. The still popular idea that to know means to be able to prove is a legacy of this tradition. Developing the implications of his starting point, Descartes regarded the reality of the physical world and of other people as matters that must be doubted until they have been established by strict demonstration. Perhaps, he suggested, all our sense experience is delusory. Perhaps, to go to the ultimate of doubt, there is an all-powerful malicious demon who not only deceives our senses but also tampers with our minds. In order to be sure that we are not being comprehensively deluded, we should therefore doubt everything that can without self-contradiction be doubted and in this way discover if anything remains immune to skepticism. There is one such indubitable item, namely, the fact that I who am now doubting exist: *cogito ergo sum* (I think, therefore I am). Building upon this immovable pinpoint of certainty, Descartes tried to establish, first the existence of God and then, through the argument that God would not allow us to be deceived, the veracity of sense perception.[1]

One of Descartes's proofs of the existence of God, the ontological argument, was discussed in Chapter 2 and found wanting. Indeed, even if that argument had seemed fully cogent, it would not have provided an escape from a self-imposed state of Cartesian doubt. For the possibility that the "malicious demon" exists and has power over our minds undermines all proofs, since that demon can (by tampering with our memories) make us believe an argument to be valid that is in fact not valid. Really radical and total doubt can never be reasoned away, since it includes even our reasoning powers within its scope. The only way of escaping such doubt is to avoid falling into it in the first place. In the present century, under the influence of G. E. Moore (1873–1958) and others, the view has gained ground that Cartesian doubt, far from being the most rational of procedures, is actually perverse and irrational. It is, Moore protested, absurd to think that we need to prove the existence of the world in which we are living. Its reality is our

---

[1]Descartes, *Discourse on Method* and *Meditations*.

paradigm of what we mean by "real." We start out with a consciousness of the world and of other people, and this consciousness is neither capable nor in need of philosophical justification.[2]

It has also been argued that when doubt becomes universal in its scope, it becomes meaningless. To doubt whether some particular perceived object is real is to doubt whether it is *as real as* the other sensible objects that we experience. "Is that chair really there?" means "Is it there in the way in which the table and the other chairs are there?" But what does it mean to doubt whether there is really anything whatever there? Such "doubt" is meaningless. For if nothing is real, there is no longer any sense in which anything can be said to be *un*real.

To pursue the same point from a slightly different perspective, if the word "real" has any meaning for us, we must acknowledge standard or paradigm cases of its correct use. We must be able to point to a clear and unproblematic instance of something's being real. What can this be but some ordinary physical object perceived by the senses? But if tables and chairs and houses and people are accepted as paradigm cases of real objects, it becomes self-contradictory to suggest that the whole world of tables and chairs and houses and people may possibly be unreal. By definition, they are not unreal, for they are typical instances of what we mean by real objects.

To deny the validity of universal skepticism of the senses is not, however, to deny that there are illusions and hallucinations, or that there are many, and perhaps even inexhaustible, philosophical problems connected with sense perception. It is one thing to know that a number of sense reports are true and another thing to arrive at their correct philosophical analysis.

This empiricist reasoning is in agreement with the unformulated epistemological assumptions of the Bible. Philosophers of the rationalist tradition, holding that to know means to be able to prove, have been shocked to find that in the Bible, which is the basis of western religion, there is no attempt to demonstrate the existence of God. Instead of professing to establish the reality of God by philosophical reasoning, the Bible takes God's reality for granted. Indeed, to the biblical writers it would have seemed absurd to try to prove by logical argument that God exists, for they were convinced that they were already having to do with God, and God with them, in all the affairs of their lives. God was known to them as a dynamic will interacting with their own wills—a sheer given reality, as inescapably to be reckoned with as destructive storm and life-giving sunshine, or the hatred of their enemies and the friendship of their neighbors. They thought of God as an experienced reality rather

[2]See G. E. Moore's papers, "The Refutation of Idealism," reprinted in *Philosophical Studies* (London: Routledge & Kegan Paul Ltd. and New York: Humanities Press, 1922); "A Defense of Common Sense," reprinted in *Philosophical Papers* (New York: The Macmillan Company and London: Allen & Unwin, 1959); and *Some Main Problems of Philosophy* (New York: The Macmillan Company and London: Allen & Unwin, 1953), Chap. 1.

than as an inferred entity. The biblical writers were (sometimes, though doubtless not at all times) as vividly conscious of being in God's presence as they were of living in a material environment. It is impossible to read their writings with any degree of sensitivity without realizing that to these people God was not a proposition completing a syllogism, or an abstract idea accepted by the mind, but the reality that gave meaning to their lives. Their pages resound and vibrate with the sense of God's presence as a building might resound and vibrate from the tread of some great being walking through it. It would be as sensible for husbands or wives to desire philosophical proof of the existence of their family members (who contribute so much to the meaning of their lives) as for persons of faith to seek proof of the existence of God, within whose purpose they are conscious that they live and move and have their being.

It is clear, then, that from the point of view of a faith that is biblical in its orientation, the traditional "theistic proofs" are religiously irrelevant. Even if God could be validly inferred from universally accepted premises, this fact would be of merely academic interest to people who believe that they exist in personal relationship with God and already know God as a living presence.

## RATIONAL BELIEF WITHOUT PROOFS

If, then, the biblical writers had also been modern epistemologists they would undoubtedly have claimed that for those who are conscious of living in the divine presence, or who experience particular events in history or in their own lives as manifestations of God's presence, it is entirely reasonable, rational, and proper to believe wholeheartedly in the reality of God. Such a religious empiricism has been present implicitly in the literature for several centuries, and explicitly throughout the present century. This theory has recently been given detailed reformulation in contemporary philosophical idiom, particularly by Alvin Plantinga and William Alston. This chapter will make use of their contributions (though without using their formal technical devices) while weaving them into a larger picture.

The issue is not whether it can be established as an item of indubitable public knowledge that God (or the Divine or the Transcendent) exists, or most probably exists, but whether it is rational for those who experience some of life's moments theistically to believe that God exists and to proceed to conduct their lives on that basis.

But we must first look at rational belief in general. "Belief" can mean a proposition believed or it can be defined as an act or state of believing. The word will be used here in both ways, though it should always be obvious which meaning is intended. But when we speak of *rational* belief we always mean, or ought to mean, a rational act or state of believing. For it is not propositions but people and their activities that can, strictly speaking, be rational or irrational. And it seems evident, indeed a tautology, that for someone rationally to believe $p$, he or she must have adequate grounds or evidence or reasons to hold that $p$ is true. To believe $p$ (if $p$ is of any importance) without basis, or for a manifestly bad reason, would not be rational. And so the nineteenth century sceptic W. K. Clifford could lay it down that "it is wrong always, everywhere, and for anyone to believe anything upon insufficient evidence."[3]

Clifford spoke of *evidence*. However, this turns out to be too narrow as a basis for rational belief. The idea of evidence normally presupposes a gap between an observed fact, or body of facts, and an inferred conclusion. Footprints are evidence that someone has passed by, but actually seeing the person pass by is not evidence of this to the observer, although her report of what she saw may be evidence for someone else. Again, if I hold my hand in front of my eyes, it is appropriate, rational, justifiable to believe that I am seeing my hand. But do I believe this on the basis of *evidence?* Surely not. What would the evidence be? Is it the visual experience of a pinkish-whitish shape, of the kind that we normally call a hand, attached within my visual field to a shape of the kind that we normally call an arm; and do I infer from this that I am seeing my hand? I am not conscious of making any such inference. Even if I did, or if I made it unconsciously, we could then ask for the evidence on which I believe that there is in my visual field this pinkish-whitish shape. And if the evidence for this is that I see it, we could ask—though with increasingly obvious absurdity—on what evidence I believe that I see it. At some point we have to accept that I just have the experience that I have, and that it is rational, appropriate, and justifiable to be in a belief–state reflecting that experience. Thus, seeing my hand, giving rise to the belief that I am seeing my hand, is an example of rational believing that is appropriately grounded in experience and yet not based upon evidence in any ordinary sense of the word. Nor does it involve any reasoning or argument because there is here no gap between premises and conclusion for reasoning to bridge.

And so our ordinary moment-to-moment perceptual beliefs contradict the principle that all rational believing must be based upon adequate evidence. It is not that they are based upon *in*adequate evidence, but rather that the model of evidence→inference→belief does not apply here. Ordinary perceptual beliefs arise directly out of our experience, and it is entirely appropriate, proper, rational to form these beliefs in this way.

Perceptual beliefs are by no means the only examples of rationally held beliefs that are not based upon evidence. Other types include believing in self-evident propositions (e.g., "there is a world"), analytic truths (e.g., "2 + 2 = 4"), and uncontroversial reports of your own memory (e.g., "I had breakfast this morning"), and also the holding of incorrigible beliefs—i.e.

[3]W. K. Clifford, "The Ethics of Belief," in *Lectures and Essays* (London: Macmillan, 1897), p. 186.

beliefs which, when sincerely held, cannot be mistaken, such as "I am now conscious" or "I feel pain in my jaw." Such beliefs, arising in us directly and not as a result of inference, are often described as basic or foundational. They are beliefs that are rational to hold in appropriate circumstances and they are grounded in and justified by those circumstances. The idea that our belief-structures are and must be built upon such basic beliefs is called *foundationalism*, although the student should be warned that the term is not always used only in precisely this way.

We can, then, reformulate Clifford's principle, not simply in terms of evidence, but more widely in terms of reasons: We should always have either appropriate experiential grounds or good reasons for our beliefs. Foundationalism adds that such "good reasons" will ultimately have to appeal to premises that are basic in the sense that they are not derived from further premises.

The various kinds of basic belief listed above fall into two groups. One consists of self-evident and analytic propositions. Believing these follows directly from understanding them; they can be basic for anyone. In these cases the differences between people's experiences do not affect their status. But in the case of perceptual and incorrigible beliefs, and those based upon memory, and again of religious beliefs, the individual's (and the community's) experience is all-important. These beliefs reflect experience, and such experience is ultimately unique to each individual. And so for such a belief to be basic is for it to be basic *for* someone. For the basicality of these beliefs is relative to the believer's range of experience or, in the cybernetic sense, information. Of course our experiences often overlap: We all see the same tree and believe on the basis of our own experience that it exists. But it is still true, for this second group of beliefs, that what counts as basic for *me* depends upon the content of *my* experience. It is this second kind of basic belief, and particularly perceptual belief, that primarily concerns us here, for it is this that provides the main analogies and disanalogies with religious belief.

Perceptual belief is basic, then, in that it is not derived from other beliefs but is directly grounded in our experience. But obviously not any and every experience can justify a basic belief, so that it exhibits, in Plantinga's phrase, proper basicality. The experience must be relevant to the belief in such a way that the belief appropriately reflects and is grounded in the experience. Further, to conclude that a belief *is* properly basic still does not establish its truth. Sense–perception beliefs, for example, although basic and although appropriately and justifiably held, can nevertheless be mistaken; for there are hallucinations, mirages, and misperceptions. Likewise memory beliefs, however uncontroversial, can also be mistaken. Thus the question whether a particular belief is basic for someone is not identical with the question whether it is *properly* basic for that person, and this in turn is not identical with the question whether the proposition believed is *true*.

How then might we establish that a properly basic belief—one that we are rationally justified in holding—is in fact true? How, for example, do we establish the truth of the perceptual belief that you see the hand that you hold before your eyes? The immediate answer is to check in obvious and familiar ways. You may turn your hand, move it further away, wiggle your fingers, and so on, and thus reassure yourself that it is indeed your hand. But such checking procedures all presuppose a more fundamental belief in the general reliability of our senses. For the appeal from a particular moment of experience to other confirming or disconfirming moments only helps if we assume that our sense experience is in general veridical, even though also subject to occasional errors. And so the ultimate question then arises: How do we know that the whole realm of sense experience is not delusory—that it consists of nothing but our own subjective states of consciousness? The answer seems to be that we cannot establish this in any noncircular way, but that it is nevertheless rational for us to assume it and to live on the basis of it; and indeed, more strongly, that it would be positively irrational not to. In other words, we have come here to something that is for us truly foundational, something that we just have to accept as a basis both for judgments about the veridical or delusory character of particular perceptions and for our thought and action generally.

We are thus led to distinguish between particular perceptual beliefs (such as the belief that a person sees a tree in front of her) and our general belief in the normally veridical rather than delusory character of sense experience. This latter is equivalent to the assumption that there is a real world of which we are a part and which impinges upon us through our sense organs. Thus if we describe as *basic* such beliefs as "I see a tree before me" (with its immediate implication that "There is a tree there"), it would be useful to have a different term for the deeper foundation on which all such beliefs rest, namely our general assumption that through our senses we are interacting with a real physical environment. Let us describe this latter belief as *foundational*.

The foundational belief in a real environment of which we are aware in sense experience is normally an unstated presupposition of our particular perceptual beliefs. It only becomes explicit when it is questioned, such questioning being of the peculiar kind that we call philosophical. Thus, as we have seen, Descartes doubted, as a thought experiment, whether anything exists other than his own consciousness; he then proceeded to reason himself, as he supposed, out of this doubt. George Berkeley argued that the material world exists only in consciousnesses, our own and God's. *Solipsism* is the theory that I alone exist and that the world and other people are modifications of my own consciousness—though it is not clear whether any sane person has ever seriously believed this. But there is, as we noted in the previous section, something peculiar about such questioning. There are no criteria of reality to which it can appeal, and further, as David Hume pointed out, we do not really have the option to disbelieve in the reality of the world in which we live, for nature "has doubtless esteem'd it an affair of too great importance to be trusted to our uncertain reasonings and speculations. We may very well ask, What causes induce us to believe in the existence of body [i.e. matter]? but 'tis vain to ask, Whether there be body or not? That is a point, which we must take for granted in all our reasonings."[4]

## BASIC RELIGIOUS BELIEFS

This distinction between basic beliefs, directly reflecting our experience, and the deeper foundational belief which they presuppose, applies also in the sphere of religion. Corresponding to the foundational belief in the reality of the physical world, of which we are aware in sense experience, is the foundational belief in the reality of the Divine, of which we are aware in religious experience. And corresponding to particular sensory beliefs, such as "I see a tree before me," are particular beliefs reflecting moments or sequences of religious experience, such as "I am conscious in this situation of being in God's presence." But the distinction between basic and foundational beliefs is more important in relation to religion than to sense experience. For whereas the foundational belief in the material world can only be artificially doubted, the parallel foundational belief in a transcendent reality or realities can be, and is, seriously doubted. We must return to this major difference, and the more specific differences that compose it, in the next section. We will concentrate now upon the particular religious beliefs that arise under the auspices of that foundational conviction. William Alston calls these "M-beliefs" ("M" for manifestation). Some of his examples of M-beliefs include "that God is speaking to [a believer], comforting him, strengthening him, enlightening him, giving him courage, guiding him, pouring out His love or joy into him, sustaining him in being."[5] We may add beliefs reflecting the sense of God's presence in moments of special joy, challenge, or tragedy, or mediated through the liturgy or the fellowship of the church, or through the beauty and grandeur of nature. Alston prefers to leave aside, because of their rare and exotic nature, the overwhelmingly powerful experiences of divine presence, and the striking visions and auditions, reported by the mystics. But these are nevertheless an important part of the continuous spectrum that runs from the faint and spasmodic moments of religious experience, punctuating the ordinary life of the believer, through the occasional "peak experiences" which come to many people, to the outstanding experiences of the classic mystics, and finally the paradigmatic experiences of the biblical figures (in the case of

---

[4]David Hume, *Treaties*, Book I, Part IV, Sec. 2, Selby-Bigge's edition (Oxford: Clarendon Press, 1896), pp. 187–88.
[5]William Alston, "Religious Experience as a Ground of Religious Belief," in *Religious Experience and Religious Belief*, eds. Joseph Runzo and Craig Ihara (Benham, Md.: University Press of America, 1987), pp. 32–33.

the Judaeo-Christian scriptures, the prophets hearing the word of the Lord or the apostles experiencing Jesus as the Christ). This spectrum flows through the various historic streams of religious experience in which individual believers participate, by which they are formed, to which they contribute, and by which they are encouraged and confirmed in their faith.

The religious beliefs based upon such M-experiences are basic in that they are not derived from other, evidence-stating, beliefs but directly reflect our own religious experience. Alvin Plantinga further argues that they are *properly* basic. That is to say, it is as rational for religious persons to hold these basic religious beliefs as it is for all of us to hold our basic perceptual beliefs. He attributes this position to the Reformers of the sixteenth century, particularly John Calvin; but, more basically, it is the biblical assumption translated into philosophical terms. That is to say, on the basis of their intense religious experiences, it was as rational for Moses and or for Jesus to believe in the reality of God as it was for them to believe in the reality of Mount Sinai or the Mount of Olives.

It is important to note that such beliefs, although not derived from other beliefs, are nevertheless not groundless. They are grounded in and justified by the experiential situation in which they have arisen. Plantinga says:

Suppose we consider perceptual beliefs, memory beliefs, and beliefs ascribing mental states to other persons, such beliefs as:

I see a tree,
I had breakfast this morning, and
That person is in pain.

Although beliefs of this sort are typically taken as basic, it would be a mistake to describe them as *groundless.* Upon having experience of a certain sort, I believe that I am perceiving a tree. In the typical case I do not hold this belief on the basis of other beliefs; it is nonetheless not groundless....We could say, if we wish, that this experience is what justifies me in holding [the belief]; this is the *ground* of my justification, and, by extension, the ground of the belief itself.[6]

He then applies this principle to religious beliefs:

Now similar things may be said about belief in God. When the Reformers claim that this belief is properly basic, they do not mean to say, of course, that there are no justifying circumstances for it, or that it is in that sense groundless or gratuitous. Quite the contrary. Calvin holds that God "reveals and daily discloses himself in the whole workmanship of the universe," and the divine art "reveals itself in the innumerable and yet distinct and well ordered variety of the heavenly host." God has so created us that we have a tendency or disposition to see his hand in the world about us. More precisely, there is in us a disposition to believe propositions of the sort *this flower was*

---

[6]"Reason and Belief in God," in *Faith and Rationality,* eds. Alvin Plantinga and Nicholas Wolterstorff (Notre Dame and London: University of Notre Dame Press, 1983), pp. 78–91.

*created by God* or *this vast and intricate universe was created by God* when we contemplate the flower or think about the vast reaches of the universe.[7]

Those who believe in God on the basis of their religious experience—experiences that they take to be of God's love, forgiveness, claim, presence, and so on—are rationally justified in so believing.

## THE FOUNDATIONAL RELIGIOUS BELIEF

The argument for the proper basicality of those religious beliefs that are grounded in religious experiences must apply not only to Christian beliefs but also to those of Judaism, Islam, Hinduism, Buddhism, and so on. (For this reason, I have used such terms as the Divine and the Transcendent as well as the specifically monotheistic term God—Buddhists and advaitic Hindus, for example, would not agree that the central religious issue is whether or not there is a personal deity.) Because of the wide differences between some of the beliefs of these traditions, and the possibility that some such beliefs are true and others false, or some more true than others, we need to distinguish between the foundational conviction that religious experience is not as such and *in toto* delusory, and the more specific beliefs that arise from the particular forms of religious experience. This distinction makes "logical space" for theories of religious pluralism (which are discussed in Chapter 9), for the dialogue of religions, and for religious criticism and doctrinal disputes. It also acknowledges the depth and seriousness of modern scepticism, which goes beyond questioning particular moments of religious experience to a rejection of the cognitive character of religious experience in general.

Religious beliefs can be challenged on two levels. On one level a particular belief is challenged because it is not consistent with our other, particularly other religious, beliefs. For example, Jim Jones's belief that he was divinely commanded to induce his followers to commit mass suicide in Jonestown in 1978 contradicts the belief in God as gracious and loving. Or again, and much more extensively, there are the disputes between followers of different religions—disputes as to whether the Ultimate Reality is personal or nonpersonal, whether the universe was created *ex nihilo* or is an emanation or is itself eternal, whether or not human beings are reincarnated, and so on. Followers of religion A reject some of the beliefs of religion B because they are inconsistent with their own A-beliefs. These controversies, conducted within a common acceptance of the foundational conviction that religious experience constitutes awareness of a transcendent divine Reality, raise difficult questions that will be addressed directly in Chapter 9.

[7]*Ibid.*, p. 80.

The second and deeper level challenges the foundational belief in the reality of God/ the Divine/ the Transcendent. This is not a religious questioning of a particular religious belief, but a nonreligious or antireligious challenge to religious belief as such. It is thus formally analogous to the philosophical doubt concerning the reality of the material world or the general validity of sense experience. But the parallel ends there. For, as we have already noted, the belief in the reality of the Transcendent is open to much more serious challenge than the purely theoretical doubt that some philosophers have professed concerning the reality of the material world. It is accordingly not sufficient to defend the foundational religious belief simply by pointing to its formal analogy with foundational perceptual belief. There are important differences suggesting that while it is reasonable to take for granted the foundational belief in the physical world, it is less reasonable, or not reasonable at all, to take for granted the foundational religious belief. For while we have no basis for doubting the existence of matter, we may have serious grounds for doubting the reality of the Divine.

William Alston has set forth the ways in which religious experience differs from sense experience. One major difference is that religious experience is not universal among human beings, whereas sense experience is. Everyone is equipped with, and no one could live without, beliefs about our physical environment. However, not everyone has, or apparently needs to have, beliefs concerning the Divine. Religious experience, and the beliefs that reflect it, seem to be optional extras, nonessential for human survival and flourishing.

A second difference is that "All normal adult human beings, whatever their culture, use basically the same conceptual scheme in objectifying their sense experience,"[8] whereas religious people are divided into groups that conceive of the Divine in very different ways. Some believe in the Holy Trinity, some in Adonai, some in Allah, some in Vishnu, some in Shiva, and yet others in the nonpersonal Brahman, or Tao, or Dharmakaya, and so on. Thus, while sense experience is roughly uniform throughout the human race, religious experience takes characteristically different forms within different religious cultures. This suggests that it may be a culturally variable human creation that we may one day no longer need, rather than a mode of experience imposed upon us by an objectively real environment.

A third difference is that (as we saw earlier) particular beliefs based upon sense perception can be checked by observation. For example, if you believe you see a tree, this can be confirmed or disconfirmed by further sense experience and also by the experience of others. The matter can usually be settled to the satisfaction of the human community—always given the general credence that we habitually give to sense experience. But in the case of religious experience there are no generally accepted checking procedures. When someone claims to have experienced a manifestation of God's presence, there is no

[8]Alston, "Religious Experience as a Ground of Religious Belief," p. 44.

accepted way in which others can confirm that this is the case. Some will be predisposed to accept the report, while others—a large majority in our modern secularized West—will sympathize with Thomas Hobbes's remark that when a man tells me that God spoke to him in a dream, this "is no more than to say he dreamed that God spake to him."[9] A skeptical reaction to a particular religious experience report will often express a general skepticism about religious experience as such.

The cumulative effect of these differences is to generate a real doubt, and not merely the peculiarly philosophical kind of doubt, about the foundational religious belief in a divine Reality to which human religious experience is a cognitive response. Seeking to counteract the effect of these differences, Alston points out that the supposed object of religious experience (which he takes in his discussion to be a personal God) may well differ from the supposed object of sense experience, namely the physical world, in ways that naturally and legitimately generate precisely these differences.

Suppose that (a) God is too different from created beings, too "wholly other," for us to be able to grasp any regularities in His behavior. Suppose further that (b) for the same reasons we can only attain the faintest, sketchiest, and most insecure grasp of what God is like. Finally, suppose that (c) God has decreed that a human being will be aware of His presence in any clear and unmistakable fashion only when certain special and difficult conditions are satisfied.[10]

The first of these three points suggests why we cannot check up on the supposed divine activity as we can on the behavior of matter. For insofar as we understand the workings of the natural world we can learn to predict changes occurring in it. In contrast to this, since we do not understand God's infinite nature, we cannot expect to predict the forms that the divine activity will take. The second point suggests why different human groups have come to conceive of and experience God in such different ways. For it could be that (as will be argued in Chapter 9) the humanly variable element in cognition naturally produces significant differences in our awareness of the Divine. Finally, the third point suggests why it is that some people do whilst others do not participate in one of the streams of religious experience. For if we are not compelled to be conscious of God, but are cognitively free in relation to our Creator, it is not surprising that at any given time some are while some are not aware of God. (See the discussion on cognitive freedom in relation to God and the notion of epistemic distance on pages 64–65.) These considerations, formulated by Alston in theistic terms, could be given analogous expression in nontheistic religious terms.

It is thus possible that religious experience differs from sense experience in just the ways that it ought to, given the fundamental differences between their

[9]*Leviathan*, Chap. 32.

[10]Alston, "Religious Experience as a Ground of Religious Belief," p. 47.

objects. These differences thus do not, in themselves, constitute a reason for denying that religious experience may be a cognitive response to a transcendent divine reality.


## THE RISK OF BELIEF

This conclusion seems thus far to be valid. That is to say, those who participate in one of the great historic streams of religious experience, accepting the body of beliefs in which it is reflected and proceeding to live on that basis, are not open to any charge of irrationality. They are, in Plantinga's phrases, not violating any epistemic duties, or forming a defective intellectual structure, but are entirely within their epistemic rights. They are, however, inevitably running a profound epistemic risk—one which is not irrational to take but of which they should be conscious.

Religious believing and disbelieving take place in a situation of ambiguity. We saw in Chapters 2 and 3 that both the main theistic and the main anti-theistic arguments are inconclusive. It is possible to think and to experience the universe, and ourselves as part of it, in both religious and naturalistic ways. For those who sometimes experience life religiously, it can be entirely rational to form beliefs reflecting that mode of experience. At the same time it is equally rational for those who do *not* participate in the field of religious experience not to hold such beliefs, and to assume that these experiences are simply projections of our human desires and ideals. (It is also possible for some who have had a religious experience to dismiss this as delusory. In contrast, others who have not had such experiences may sometimes be so impressed by the лives of outstanding believers that they also come to believe in the reality of the Divine.)

It is however another feature of our situation that (as will be argued more fully in Chapter 8) if the universe is, after all, religiously structured, this will ultimately be confirmed within our experience. In other words, we are facing an issue of fact which is at present veiled in ambiguity, so that both belief and disbelief at present carry with them the risk of profound error. The believer risks the possibility of being deluded and of living, as a result, in a state of self-deception. The nonbeliever risks the possibility of shutting out the most valuable of all realities.

Let us now concentrate upon the believer who acknowledges the present religious ambiguity of the universe. Such a person may find warrant for taking this risk in a revision of William James's "right to believe" argument. We looked at James's own version of this in the last chapter and concluded that as it stands it is altogether too permissive. The only ground for belief that James offers is an inclination or desire to believe. He claims that if we have such an inclination, we are entitled to believe accordingly. But this would validate any and every belief that anyone feels an inclination to hold, so long as it is not capable of being proved or disproved. In the light of the previous discussion, a more acceptable justification is provided by religious experience. Let us then reformulate James's argument as follows. The practical question is whether or not to trust our religious experience as an authentic awareness of the Divine. We have seen that it is rationally permissible either to trust or to distrust it. Each option carries with it momentous consequences. For one must risk either, if disbelief turns out to be misplaced, missing a great good, indeed the greatest of all goods; or on the other hand, if belief turns out to be misplaced, falling into the most pathetic of delusions. Given this choice James would urge, and surely with reason, that we have the right to choose for ourselves. People are therefore justified in holding beliefs that are grounded either wholly in their own religious experience or in the experience of the historical tradition to which they belong, this being in turn confirmed by their own much slighter range and intensity of religious experience.

Of course, the options may not be quite so final as James sometimes seemed to assume, and as Pascal (see page 59) certainly supposed, namely as leading to eternal gain or loss. If the universe is religiously structured in a way that will eventually become evident to everyone, it seems likely that all will eventually become oriented to the divine Reality—or, in traditional theological language, will attain to eternal life. The "missing a great good, indeed the greatest of all goods" will then only be temporary, even though it may last for the remainder of this present life. In that case, what is missed now by the nonbeliever is the present good of a conscious relationship to the divine Reality and a life lived in that relationship. But we must add that in our present situation of ambiguity a balancing danger is incurred by the believer. For if in fact mistaken, the believer has fallen into the indignity of failing to face the harsh reality of our human situation and of embracing instead a comforting illusion. It seems that we stand, as finite and ignorant beings, in a universe that both invites religious belief and yet holds over us the possibility that this invitation may be a deception!

# CHAPTER 7

# Problems of Religious Language

## THE PECULIARITY OF RELIGIOUS LANGUAGE

Modern work in the philosophy of religion has been much occupied with problems created by the distinctively religious uses of language. The discussions generally center around one of two main issues. One, which was familiar to medieval thinkers, concerns the special sense that descriptive terms bear when they are applied to God. The other question, which also has a long history but which has been given fresh sharpness and urgency by contemporary analytical philosophy, is concerned with the basic function of religious language. In particular, do those religious statements that have the form of factual assertions (for example, "God loves humankind") refer to a special kind of fact—religious as distinguished from scientific fact—or do they fulfill a different function altogether? These questions will be discussed in the order in which they have just been mentioned.

It is obvious that many, perhaps all, of the terms that are applied in religious discourse to God are being used in special ways, differing from their use in ordinary mundane contexts. For example, when it is said that "Great is the Lord," it is not meant that God occupies a large volume of space; when it is said that "the Lord spake unto Joshua," it is not meant that God has a physical body with speech organs which set in motion sound waves which impinged upon Joshua's eardrums. When it is said that God is good, it is not meant that there are moral values independent of the divine nature, in relation to which God can be judged to be good; nor does it mean (as it commonly does of human beings) that God is subject to temptations but succeeds in overcoming them.

There has clearly been a long shift of meaning between the familiar secular use of these words and their theological employment.

It is also clear that in all those cases in which a word occurs both in secular and in theological contexts, its secular meaning is primary, in the sense that it developed first and has accordingly determined the definition of the word. The meaning that such a term bears when it is applied to God is an adaptation of its secular use. Consequently, although the ordinary, everyday meaning of such words as "good," "loving," "forgives," "commands," "hear," "speaks," "wills," and "purposes" is relatively unproblematic, the same terms raise a multitude of questions when applied to God. To take a single example, love (whether *eros* or *agape*) is expressed in behavior in the speaking of words of love, and in a range of actions from lovemaking to the various forms of practical and sacrificial caring. But God is said to be "without body, parts, or passions." God has then, it would seem, no local existence or bodily presence through which to express love. But what is disembodied love, and how can we ever know that it exists? Parallel questions arise in relation to the other divine attributes.

## THE DOCTRINE OF ANALOGY (AQUINAS)

The great Scholastic thinkers were well aware of this problem and developed the idea of analogy to meet it. The doctrine of "analogical predication" as it occurs in Aquinas[1] and his commentator Cajetan,[2] and as it has been further elaborated and variously criticized in modern times, is too complex a subject to be discussed in detail within the plan of this book. However, Aquinas's basic and central idea is not difficult to grasp. He teaches that when a word such as "good" is applied both to a created being and to God, it is not being used *univocally* (that is, with exactly the same meaning) in the two cases. God is not good in identically the sense in which human beings may be good. Nor, on the other hand, do we apply the epithet "good" to God and humans *equivocally* (that is, with completely different and unrelated meanings), as when the word "bat" is used to refer both to the flying animal and to the thing used in baseball. There is a definite connection between divine and human goodness, reflecting the fact that God has created humankind. According to Aquinas, then, "good" is applied to creator and creature neither univocally nor equivocally but *analogically*. What this means will appear if we consider first an analogy "downwards" from humanity to a lower form of life. We sometimes say of a pet dog that it is faithful, and we may also describe a man or a woman as faithful. We use the same word in each case because of a

---

[1] *Summa Theologica*, Part I, Question 13, Art. 5; *Summa Contra Gentiles*, Book 1, Chaps. 28–34.

[2] Thomas De Vio, Cardinal Cajetan, *The Analogy of Names*, 1506, 2nd ed. (Pittsburgh: Duquesne University Press, 1959).

similarity between a certain quality exhibited in the behavior of the dog and the steadfast voluntary adherence to a person or a cause that we call faithfulness in a human being. Because of this similarity, we are not using the word "faithful" equivocally (with totally different senses.) On the other hand, there is an immense difference in quality between a dog's attitudes and a person's. The one is indefinitely superior to the other in respect of responsible, self-conscious deliberation and the relating of attitudes to moral purposes and ends. Because of this difference, we are not using "faithful" univocally (in exactly the same sense). We are using it analogically, to indicate that at the level of the dog's consciousness there is a quality that *corresponds* to what at the human level we call faithfulness. There is a recognizable likeness in structure of attitudes or patterns of behavior that causes us to use the same word for both animals and people. Nevertheless, human faithfulness differs from canine faithfulness to all the wide extent that a person differs from a dog. There is thus both similarity within difference and difference within similarity of the kind that led Aquinas to speak of the *analogical* use of the same term in two very different contexts.

In the case of our analogy downwards, true or normative faithfulness is that which we know directly in ourselves, and the dim and imperfect faithfulness of the dog is known only by analogy. However, in the case of the analogy upwards from humanity to God the situation is reversed. It is our own directly known goodness, love, wisdom, and so on that are the thin shadows and remote approximations, and the perfect qualities of the Godhead that are known to us only by analogy. Thus, when we say that God is good, we are saying that there is a quality of the infinitely perfect Being that corresponds to what at our own human level we call goodness. In this case, it is the divine goodness that is the true, normative, and unbroken reality, whereas human life shows at best a faint, fragmentary, and distorted reflection of this quality. Only in God can the perfections of being occur in their true and unfractured nature: only God knows, loves, and is righteous and wise in the full and proper sense.

Since the deity is hidden from us, the question arises of how we can know what goodness and the other divine attributes are in God. How do we know what perfect goodness and wisdom are like? Aquinas's answer is that we do not know. As used by him, the doctrine of analogy does not profess to spell out the concrete character of God's perfections, but only to indicate the relation between the different meanings of a word when it is applied both to humanity and (on the basis of revelation) to God. Analogy is not an instrument for exploring and mapping the infinite divine nature; it is an account of the way in which terms are used of the Deity whose existence is, at this point, being presupposed. The doctrine of analogy provides a framework for certain limited statements about God without infringing upon the agnosticism, and the sense of the mystery of the divine being, which have always characterized Christian and Jewish thought at their best.

The conviction that it is possible to talk about God, yet that such talk can be carried to its destination only on the back of the distant analogy between the Creator and his creatures, is vividly expressed by the Catholic lay theologian, Baron von Hügel (1852–1925).[3] He speaks of the faint, dim, and confused awareness that a dog has of its master, and continues as follows:

The source and object of religion, if religion be true and its object be real, *cannot* indeed, *by any possibility, be as clear to me even as I am to my dog*. For the cases we have considered deal with realities inferior to our own reality (material objects, or animals), or with realities level to our own reality (fellow human beings), or with realities no higher above ourselves than are we, finite human beings, to our very finite dogs. Whereas, in the case of religion—if religion be right—we apprehend and affirm realities indefinitely superior in quality and amount of reality to ourselves, and which, nevertheless (or rather, just because of this), anticipate, penetrate, and sustain us with a quite unpicturable intimacy. The obscurity of my life to my dog, must thus be greatly exceeded by the obscurity of the life of God to me. Indeed the obscurity of plant life—so obscure for my mind, because so indefinitely inferior and poorer than is my human life—must be greatly exceeded by the dimness, for my human life, of God—of His reality and life, so different and superior, so unspeakably more rich and alive, than is, or ever can be, my own life and reality.[4]

## RELIGIOUS STATEMENTS AS SYMBOLIC (TILLICH)

An important element in the thought of Paul Tillich is his doctrine of the "symbolic" nature of religious language.[5] Tillich distinguishes between a sign and a symbol. Both point to something else beyond themselves. But a sign signifies that to which it points by arbitrary convention—as for instance, when the red light at the street corner signifies that drivers are ordered to halt. In contrast to this purely external connection, a symbol "participates in that to which it points."[6] To use Tillich's example, a flag participates in the power

[3]Friedrich von Hügel's principal works are *The Mystical Element in Religion* and *Eternal Life*, and the two volumes of *Essays and Addresses on the Philosophy of Religion*, each of which is a major classic on its subject.

[4]Friedrich von Hügel, *Essays and Addresses on the Philosophy of Religion*, First Series (New York: E. P. Dutton & Co., Inc. and London: J. M. Dent & Sons Ltd., 1921), pp. 102–3.

[5]This is to be found in Tillich's *Systematic Theology* and *Dynamics of Faith*, and in a number of articles: "The Religious Symbol," *Journal of Liberal Religion*, II, No. 1 (Summer 1940); "Religious Symbols and our Knowledge of God," *The Christian Scholar*, XXXVIII, No. 3 (September 1955); "Theology and Symbolism," *Religious Symbolism*, ed. F. E. Johnson (New York: Harper & Row, Publishers, 1955); "Existential Analyses and Religious Symbols," *Contemporary Problems in Religion*, ed. Harold A. Basilius (Detroit: Wayne State University Press, 1956), reprinted in *Four Existentialist Theologians*, ed. Will Herberg (Garden City, N.Y.: Doubleday & Company, Inc., Anchor Books, 1958); "The Word of God," *Language*, ed. Ruth Anshen (New York: Harper & Row, Publishers, 1957). For a philosophical critique of Tillich's doctrine of religious symbols, see William Alston, "Tillich's Conception of a Religious Symbol," *Religious Experience and Truth*, ed. Sidney Hook (New York: New York University Press, 1961), which volume also contains two further essays by Tillich, "The Religious Symbol" and "The Meaning and Justification of Religious Symbols."

[6]Paul Tillich, *Dynamics of Faith* (New York: Harper & Row, Publishers), p. 42.

and dignity of the nation that it represents. Because of this inner connection with the reality symbolized, symbols are not arbitrarily instituted, like conventional signs, but "grow out of the individual or collective unconscious"[7] and consequently have their own span of life and (in some cases) their decay and death. A symbol "opens up levels of reality which otherwise are closed to us" and at the same time "unlocks dimensions and elements of our soul"[8] corresponding to the new aspects of the world that it reveals. The clearest instances of this twofold function are provided by the arts, which "create symbols for a level of reality which cannot be reached in any other way,"[9] at the same time opening up new sensitivities and powers of appreciation in ourselves.

Tillich holds that religious faith, which is the state of being "ultimately concerned" about the ultimate, can express itself only in symbolic language. "Whatever we say about that which concerns us ultimately, whether or not we call it God, has a symbolic meaning. It points beyond itself while participating in that to which it points. In no other way can faith express itself adequately. The language of faith is the language of symbols."[10]

There is, according to Tillich, one and only one literal, nonsymbolic statement that can be made about the ultimate reality which religion calls God— that God is Being-itself. Beyond this, all theological statements—such as that God is eternal, living, good, personal, that God is the Creator and that God loves all creatures—are symbolic:

There can be no doubt that any concrete assertion about God must be symbolic, for a concrete assertion is one which uses a segment of finite experience in order to say something about him. It transcends the content of this segment, although it also includes it. The segment of finite reality which becomes the vehicle of a concrete assertion about God is affirmed and negated at the same time. It becomes a symbol, for a symbolic expression is one whose proper meaning is negated by that to which it points. And yet it also is affirmed by it, and this affirmation gives the symbolic expression an adequate basis for pointing beyond itself.[11]

Tillich's conception of the symbolic character of religious language can— like many of his central ideas—be developed in either of two opposite directions, and it is presented by Tillich in the body of his writings as a whole in such a way as to preserve its ambiguity and flexibility. We shall, at this point, consider Tillich's doctrine in its theistic development, indicating in a later

[7]*Ibid.*, p. 43.
[8]*Ibid.*, p. 42.
[9]*Ibid.*, p. 42.
[10]*Ibid.*, p. 45.
[11]Tillich, *Systematic Theology*, I, 239.

section, in connection with the view of J. H. Randall, Jr., how it can also be developed naturalistically.[12]

Used in the service of Judaic-Christian theism, the negative aspect of Tillich's doctrine of religious symbols corresponds to the negative aspect of the doctrine of analogy. Tillich is insisting that we do not use human language literally, or univocally, when we speak of the ultimate. Because our terms can only be derived from our own finite human experience, they cannot be adequate in relation to God; when they are used theologically, their meaning is always partially "negated by that to which they point." Religiously, this doctrine constitutes a warning against the idolatry of thinking of God as merely a greatly magnified human being (anthropomorphism).

Tillich's constructive teaching, offering an alternative to the doctrine of analogy, is his theory of "participation." A symbol, he says, participates in the reality to which it points. Unfortunately Tillich does not fully define or clarify this central notion of participation. Consider, for example, the symbolic statement that God is good. Is the symbol in this case the proposition "God is good," or the concept "the goodness of God"? Does this symbol participate in Being-itself in the same sense as that in which a flag participates in the power and dignity of a nation? And what precisely is this sense? Tillich does not analyze the latter case—which he uses in several places to indicate what he means by the participation of a symbol in that which it symbolizes. Consequently, it is not clear in what respect the case of a religious symbol is supposed to be similar. Again, according to Tillich, everything that exists participates in Being-itself; what then is the difference between the way in which symbols participate in Being-itself and the way in which everything else participates in it?

The application to theological statements of Tillich's other "main characteristics of every symbol,"[13] summarized above, raises further questions. Is it really plausible to say that a complex theological statement such as "God is not dependent for his existence upon any external reality" has arisen from the unconscious, whether individual or collective? Does it not seem more likely that it was carefully formulated by a philosophical theologian? And in what sense does this same proposition open up both "levels of reality which are otherwise closed to us" and "hidden depths of our own being"? These two characteristics of symbols seem more readily applicable to the arts than to theological ideas and propositions. Indeed, it is Tillich's tendency to assimilate religious to aesthetic awareness that suggests the naturalistic development of his position, which will be described later (pp. 89–91).

[12]See pp. 89–91.
[13]Tillich, *Dynamics of Faith*, p. 43.

These are some of the many questions that Tillich's position raises. In default of answers to such questions, Tillich's teaching, although valuably suggestive, scarcely constitutes at this point a fully articulated philosophical position.

## INCARNATION AND THE PROBLEM OF MEANING

It is claimed by some that the doctrine of the Incarnation (which together with all that follows from it distinguishes Christianity from Judaism) offers the possibility of a partial solution to the problem of theological meaning. There is a longstanding distinction between the metaphysical attributes of God (aseity, eternity, infinity, etc.) and God's moral attributes (goodness, love, wisdom, etc.). The doctrine of the Incarnation involves the claim that the moral (but not the metaphysical) attributes of God have been embodied, so far as this is possible, in a finite human life, namely that of Jesus. This claim makes it possible to point to the person of Christ as showing what is meant by assertions such as "God is good" and "God loves his human creatures." The moral attitudes of God toward humanity are held to have been incarnated in Jesus and expressed concretely in his dealings with men and women. The Incarnation doctrine involves the claim that, for example, Jesus' compassion for the sick and the spiritually blind was God's compassion for them; his forgiving of sins, God's forgiveness; and his condemnation of the self-right-eously religious, God's condemnation of them. On the basis of this belief, the life of Christ as depicted in the New Testament provides a foundation for statements about God. From God's attitudes in Christ toward a random assortment of men and women in first-century Palestine, it is possible to affirm, for example, that God's love is continuous in character with that displayed in the life of Jesus.[14]

The doctrine of the Incarnation is used in relation to the same problem in a somewhat different way by Ian Crombie. "What we do [he says in the course of an illuminating discussion of the problem of theological meaning] is in essence to think of God in parables." He continues as follows:

The things we say about God are said on the authority of the words and acts of Christ, who spoke in human language, using parable; and so we too speak of God in parable—authoritative parable, authorized parable; knowing that the truth is not literally that which our parables represent, knowing therefore that now we see in a glass darkly, but trusting, because we trust the source of the parables, that in believing them and interpreting them in the light of each other we shall not be misled, that we shall have such knowledge as we need to possess for the foundation of the religious life.[15]

[14]For a criticism of this view, see Ronald Hepburn, *Christianity and Paradox* (London: C. A. Watts & Co., Ltd., 1958, and Indianapolis: The Bobbs-Merrill Co., Inc., 1968), Chap. 5.

[15]Ian Crombie, "Theology and Falsification," *New Essays in Philosophical Theology*, eds. Antony Flew and Alasdair MacIntyre (London: S.C.M. Press and New York: Macmillan, 1955), pp. 122–23. See also Ian Crombie's article, "The Possibility of Theological Statements" in *Faith and Logic*, ed. Basil Mitchell (London: George Allen & Unwin Ltd., 1957).

## RELIGIOUS LANGUAGE AS NONCOGNITIVE

When we assert what we take to be a fact (or deny what is alleged to be a fact), we are using language cognitively. "The population of China is one billion," "This is a hot summer," "Two plus two equal four," "He is not here" are cognitive utterances. Indeed, we can define a cognitive (or informative or indicative) sentence as one that is either true or false.

There are, however, other types of utterance which are neither true nor false because they fulfill a different function from that of endeavoring to describe facts. We do not ask of a swearword, or a command, or the baptismal formula whether it is true. The function of the swearword is to vent one's feelings; of the command, to direct someone's actions; of "I baptize thee...," to perform a baptism. The question arises whether theological sentences such as "God loves humankind" are cognitive or noncognitive. This query at once divides into two: (1) Are such sentences intended by their users to be construed cognitively? (2) Is their logical character such that they can, in fact, regardless of intention, be either true or false? The first of these questions will be discussed in the present and the second in the following chapter.

There is no doubt that as a matter of historical fact religious people have normally believed such statements as "God loves humanity" to be not only cognitive but also true. Without necessarily pausing to consider the difference between religious facts and the facts disclosed through sense perception and the sciences, ordinary believers within the Judaic-Christian tradition have assumed that there are religious realities and facts and that their own religious convictions are concerned with such.

Today, however, a growing number of theories treat religious language as noncognitive. Three of these theories, of somewhat different types, will be described in this and the next two sections. A clear statement of the first type comes from J. H. Randall, Jr. in his book, *The Role of Knowledge in Western Religion.*[16] His exposition indicates, incidentally, how a view of religious symbols that is very close to Tillich's can be used in the service of naturalism.[17]

Randall conceives of religion as a human activity which, like its compeers, science and art, makes its own special contribution to human culture. The distinctive material with which religion works is a body of symbols and myths. "What is important to recognize [says Randall] is that religious symbols belong with social and artistic symbols, in the group of symbols that are both *nonrepresentative* and *noncognitive*. Such noncognitive symbols can be

[16]J. H. Randall, Jr., *The Role of Knowledge in Western Religion* (Boston: Beacon Press, 1958).

[17]Randall himself, in a paper published in 1954, in which he presented the same theory of religious language, said, "The position I am here trying to state I have been led to work out in connection with various courses on myths and symbols I have given jointly with Paul Tillich....After long discussions, Mr. Tillich and I have found we are very close to agreement." *The Journal of Philosophy,* LI, No. 5 (March 4, 1954), 159. Tillich's article that develops his doctrine of symbols most clearly in the direction taken by Randall is "Religious Symbols and Our Knowledge of God," *The Christian Scholar* (September 1955).

said to symbolize not some external thing that can be indicated apart from their operation, but rather what they themselves *do*, their peculiar functions."[18]

According to Randall, religious symbols have a fourfold function. First, they arouse the emotions and stir people to actions; they may thereby strengthen people's practical commitment to what they believe to be right. Second, they stimulate cooperative action and thus bind a community together through a common response to its symbols. Third, they are able to communicate qualities of experience that cannot be expressed by the literal use of language. Fourth, they both evoke and serve to foster and clarify our human experience of an aspect of the world that can be called the "order of splendor" or the Divine. In describing this last function of religious symbols, Randall develops an aesthetic analogy:

The work of the painter, the musician, the poet, teaches us how to use our eyes, our ears, our minds, and our feelings with greater power and skill....It shows us how to discern unsuspected qualities in the world encountered, latent powers and possibilities there resident. Still more, it makes us see the new qualities with which the world, in cooperation with the spirit of man, can clothe itself....Is it otherwise with the prophet and the saint? They too can do something to us, they too can effect changes in us and in our world....They teach us how to see what man's life in the world is, and what it might be. They teach us how to discern what human nature can make out of its natural conditions and materials....They make us receptive to qualities of the world encountered; and they open our hearts to the new qualities with which that world, in cooperation with the spirit of man, can clothe itself. They enable us to see and feel the religious dimension of our world better, the "order of splendor," and of man's experience in and with it. They teach us how to find the Divine; they show us visions of God.[19]

It is to be noted that Randall's position represents a radical departure from the traditional assumptions of Western religion, for in speaking of "finding the Divine" and of being shown "visions of God," Randall does not mean to imply that God or the Divine exists as a reality independent of the human mind. He is speaking "symbolically." God is "our ideals, our controlling values, our 'ultimate concern,' "[20] he is "an intellectual symbol for the religious dimension of the world, for the Divine."[21] This religious dimension is "a quality to be discriminated in human experience of the world, the splendor of the vision that sees beyond the actual into the perfected and eternal realm of the imagination."[22] This last statement, however, is enlivened by a philosophic rhetoric which may unintentionally obscure underlying issues. The

---

[18]J. H. Randall, Jr., *The Role of Knowledge in Western Religion* (Boston: Beacon Press, 1958), p. 114. Reprinted by permission of the author.

[19]*Ibid.*, pp. 128–29.

[20]*Ibid.*, p. 33.

[21]*Ibid.*, p. 112.

[22]*Ibid.*, p. 119.

products of the human imagination are not eternal; they did not exist before men and women themselves existed, and they can persist, even as imagined entities, only as long as men and women exist. The Divine, as defined by Randall, is the temporary mental construction or projection of a recently emerged animal inhabiting one of the satellites of a minor star. God is not, according to this view, the creator and the ultimate ruler of the universe; God is a fleeting ripple of imagination in a tiny corner of space-time.

Randall's theory of religion and of the function of religious language expresses with great clarity a way of thinking that in less clearly defined forms is widespread today and is, indeed, characteristic of our culture. This way of thinking is epitomized in the way in which the word "religion" (or "faith" used virtually as a synonym) has largely come to replace the word "God." In contexts in which formerly questions were raised and debated concerning God, God's existence, attributes, purpose, and deeds, the corresponding questions today typically concern religion, its nature, function, forms, and pragmatic value. A shift has taken place from the term "God" as the head of a certain group of words and locutions to the term "religion" as the new head of the same linguistic family.

There is, accordingly, much discussion of religion considered as an aspect of human culture. As Randall says, "Religion, we now see, is a distinctive human enterprise with a socially indispensable function of its own to per-form."[23] In many universities and colleges there are departments devoted to studying the history and varieties of this phenomenon and the contribution that it has brought to our culture in general. Among the ideas treated in this connection, along with cult, priesthood, taboo, and many others, is the concept of God. For academic study, God is thus conceived as a subtopic within the larger subject of religion.

At a more popular level religion is widely regarded, in a psychological mode, as a human activity whose general function is to enable the individual to achieve harmony both internally and in relation to the environment. One of the distinctive ways in which religion fulfills this function is by preserving and promoting certain great ideas or symbols that possess the power to invigorate our finer aspirations. The most important and enduring of these symbols is God. Thus, at both academic and popular levels God is, in effect, defined in terms of religion, as one of the concepts with which religion works, rather than religion being defined in terms of God, as the field of people's varying responses to a real supernatural being.

This displacement of "God" by "Religion" as the focus of a wide realm of discourse has brought with it a change in the character of the questions that are most persistently asked in this area. Concerning God, the traditional question has naturally been whether God exists or is real. This is not a question

---

[23]*Ibid.*, p. 6.

that arises with regard to religion. It is obvious that religion exists; the important queries concern the purposes that it serves in human life, whether it ought to be cultivated, and if so, in what directions it may most profitably be developed. Under the pressure of these concerns, the question of the truth of religious beliefs has fallen into the background and the issue of their practical usefulness has come forward instead to occupy the center of attention.

In the perspective of history, is this pragmatic emphasis a surrogate for the older conception of objective religious realities, a substitute natural to an age of waning faith? Such a diagnosis is suggested by the observations of the agnostic, John Stuart Mill, in his famous essay on *The Utility of Religion:*

If religion, or any particular form of it, is true, its usefulness follows without other proof. If to know authentically in what order of things, under what government of the universe it is our destiny to live, were not useful, it is difficult to imagine what could be considered so. Whether a person is in a pleasant or in an unpleasant place, a palace or a prison, it cannot be otherwise than useful to him to know where he is. So long, therefore, as men accepted the teachings of their religion as positive facts, no more a matter of doubt than their own existence or the existence of the objects around them, to ask the use of believing it could not possibly occur to them. The utility of religion did not need to be asserted until the arguments for its truth had in a great measure ceased to convince. People must either have ceased to believe, or have ceased to rely on the belief of others, before they could take that inferior ground of defence without a consciousness of lowering what they were endeavouring to raise. An argument for the utility of religion is an appeal to unbelievers, to induce them to practice a well meant hypocrisy, or to semi-believers to make them avert their eyes from what might possibly shake their unstable belief, or finally to persons in general to abstain from expressing any doubts they may feel, since a fabric of immense importance to mankind is so insecure at its foundations that men must hold their breath in its neighbourhood for fear of blowing it down.[24]

Comparing this current emphasis upon utility rather than truth with the thought of the great biblical exemplars of faith, we are at once struck by a startling reversal. There is a profound difference between serving and worshiping God and being "interested in religion." God, if God is real, is our Creator, infinitely superior to ourselves, in worth as well as in power, One "in whose eyes all hearts are open, all desires known, and from whom no secrets are hid." On the other hand, religion stands before us as one of the various concerns that we may, at our own option, choose to pursue. In dealing with religion and the religions, we occupy the appraiser's role, and God is subsumed within that which we appraise. There need be no baring of one's life before divine judgment and mercy. We can deal instead with religion, within which God is an idea, a concept whose history we can trace, and which we can analyze, define, and even revise. God is not, as in biblical thought, the

---

[24]J. S. Mill, *Three Essays on Religion* (London: Longmans, 1875, and Westport, Conn.: Greenwood Press), pp. 69–70.

living Lord of heaven and earth before whom men and women bow down in awe to worship and rise up with joy to serve.

The historical sources of the now prevalent and perhaps even dominant view of religion as essentially an aspect of human culture are fairly evident. This view of religion represents a logical development, within an increasingly technological society, of what has been variously called scientism, positivism, and naturalism. This development is based upon the assumption—engendered by the tremendous, dramatic, and still accelerating growth of scientific knowledge and achievement—that the truth concerning any aspect or alleged aspect of reality is to be found by the application of scientific methods to the relevant phenomena. God is not a phenomenon available for scientific study, but religion is. There can be a history, a phenomenology, a psychology, a sociology, and a comparative study of religion. Hence, religion has become an object of intensive investigation and God is perforce identified as an idea that occurs within this complex phenomenon of religion.

## BRAITHWAITE'S NONCOGNITIVE THEORY

A second theory of the function of religion that asserts the noncognitive character of religious language was offered by R. B. Braithwaite.[25] He suggests that religious assertions serve primarily an ethical function. The purpose of ethical statements is, according to Braithwaite, to express the speaker's adherence to a certain policy of action; they express "the intention of the asserter to act in a particular sort of way specified in the assertion…when a man asserts that he ought to do so-and-so, he is using the assertion to declare that he resolves, to the best of his ability, to do so-and-so."[26] Thereby, of course, the speaker also recommends this way of behaving to others. Religious statements, likewise, express and recommend a commitment to a certain general policy or way of life. For example, a Christian's assertion that God is love (*agape*) is the speaker's indication of "intention to follow an agapeistic way of life."[27]

---

[25]R. B. Braithwaite, *An Empiricist's View of the Nature of Religious Belief* (Cambridge: Cambridge University Press and Folcroft, Pa.: Folcroft Library Editions, 1955). Reprinted in *The Existence of God*, ed. John Hick (New York: The Macmillan Company, 1964), and *Classical and Contemporary Readings in the Philosophy of Religion*, ed. J. Hick (Englewood Cliffs, N.J.: Prentice-Hall, Inc., 1989). Other philosophers who have independently developed noncognitive analyses of religious language that show a family resemblance to that of Braithwaite are Peter Munz, *Problems of Religious Knowledge* (London: Student Christian Movement Press Ltd., 1959); T. R. Miles, *Religion and the Scientific Outlook* (London: George Allen & Unwin Ltd., 1959); Paul F. Schmidt, *Religious Knowledge* (New York: The Free Press, 1961); Paul Van Buren, *The Secular Meaning of the Gospel* (New York: The Macmillan Company, 1963); and Don Cupitt, *Taking Leave of God* (London: S.C.M. Press, 1980), *The World to Come* (London: S.C.M. Press, 1982), and *Only Human* (London: S.C.M. Press, 1985).

[26]Braithwaite, *Nature of Religious Belief*, pp. 12–14.

[27]*Ibid.*, p. 18.

Braithwaite next raises the question: when two religions (say Christianity and Buddhism) recommend essentially the same policy for living, in what sense are they different religions? There are, of course, wide divergences of ritual, but these, in Braithwaite's view, are relatively unimportant. The significant distinction lies in the different sets of stories (or myths or parables) that are associated in the two religions with adherence to their way of life.

It is not necessary, according to Braithwaite, that these stories be true or even that they be believed to be true. The connection between religious stories and the religious way of life is "a psychological and causal one. It is an empirical psychological fact that many people find it easier to resolve upon and to carry through a course of action which is contrary to their natural inclinations if this policy is associated in their minds with certain stories. And in many people the psychological link is not appreciably weakened by the fact that the story associated with the behavior policy is not believed. Next to the Bible and the Prayer Book the most influential work in English Christian religious life has been a book whose stories are frankly recognized as fictitious—Bunyan's *Pilgrim's Progress*."[28]

In summary, Braithwaite states, "A religious assertion, for me, is the assertion of an intention to carry out a certain behavior policy, subsumable under a sufficiently general principle to be a moral one, together with the implicit or explicit statement, but not the assertion, of certain stories."[29]

Some questions may now be raised for discussion.

1. As in the case of Randall's theory, Braithwaite considers religious statements to function in a way that is different from the way they have, in fact, been used by the great majority of religious persons. In Braithwaite's form of Christianity, God has the status of a character in the associated fictional stories.

2. The ethical theory upon which Braithwaite bases his account of religious language holds that moral assertions are expressions of the asserter's intention to act in the way specified in the assertion. For example, "Lying is wrong" means "I intend never to lie." If this were so, it would follow that it would be logically impossible to *intend* to act wrongly. "Lying is wrong, but I intend to tell a lie" would be a sheer contradiction, equivalent to "I intend never to lie (= lying is wrong) but I intend to lie." This consequence conflicts with the way in which we actually speak in ethical contexts; sometimes people *do* knowingly intend to act wrongly.

3. The Christian stories to which Braithwaite refers in the course of his lecture are of very diverse logical types. They include straightforward historical statements about the life of Jesus, mythological expressions of belief in creation and a final judgment, and belief in the existence of God. Of these, only the first category appears to fit Braithwaite's own definition of a story as "a

---

[28]*Ibid.*, p. 27.
[29]*Ibid.*, p. 32.

proposition or set of propositions which are straightforwardly empirical propositions capable of empirical test."[30] Statements such as "God was in Christ reconciling the world to himself" or "God loves humankind" do not constitute stories in Braithwaite's sense. Thus, his category of religious stories takes account only of one relatively peripheral type of religious statement; it is unable to accommodate those central, more directly and distinctively religious statements that refer to God. To a great extent it is people's beliefs about God that impel them to an agapeistic way of life. Yet, these most important beliefs remain unanalyzed, for they cannot be placed in the only category that Braithwaite supplies, that of unproblematically factual beliefs.

4. Braithwaite holds that beliefs about God are relevant to a person's practical behavior because they provide it with psychological reinforcement. However, another possible view of the matter is that the ethical significance of these beliefs consists of the way in which they render a certain way of life both attractive and rational. This view would seem to be consistent with the character of Jesus' ethical teaching. He did not demand that people live in a way that runs counter to their deepest desires and that would thus require some extraordinary counterbalancing inducement. Rather, he professed to reveal to them the true nature of the world in which they live, and in the light of this, to indicate the way in which their deepest desires might be fulfilled. In an important sense, then, Jesus did not propose any new motive for action. He did not set up a new end to be sought, or a new impulse toward an already familiar end. Instead, he offered a new vision or mode of apperceiving the world, such that to live rationally in the world as thus seen is to live in the kind of way he described. He sought to replace the various attitudes and policies for living which express the sense of insecurity that is natural enough if the world really is an arena of competing interests, in which each must safeguard oneself and one's own against the rival egoisms of one's neighbors. If human life is essentially a form of animal life, and human civilization a refined jungle in which self-concern operates more subtly, but not less surely, than animal tooth and claw, then the quest for invulnerability in its many guises is entirely rational. To seek security in the form of power over others, whether physical, psychological, economic, or political, or in the form of recognition and acclaim, would then be indicated by the terms of the human situation. Jesus, however, rejected these attitudes and objectives as being based upon an estimate of the world that is false because it is atheistic; it assumes that there is no God, or at least none such as Jesus knew. Jesus was far from being an idealist if by this we mean one who sets up ideals unrelated to the facts and who recommends that we be guided by them rather than by the realities of our lives. On the contrary, Jesus was a realist; he pointed to the life in which the neighbor is valued equally with the self as being indicated

[30]*Ibid.*, p. 23.

by the actual nature of the universe. He urged people to live in terms of reality. His morality differed from normal human practice because his view of reality differed from our normal view of the world. Whereas the ethic of egoism is ultimately atheistic, Jesus' ethic was radically and consistently theistic. It sets forth the way of life that is appropriate when God, as depicted by Jesus, is wholeheartedly believed to be real. The pragmatic and in a sense prudential basis of Jesus' moral teaching is very clearly expressed in his parable of the two houses built on sand and on rock.[31] The parable claims that the universe is so constituted that to live in the way Jesus has described is to build one's life upon enduring foundations, whereas to live in the opposite way is to go "against the grain" of things and to court ultimate disaster. The same thought occurs in the saying about the two ways, one of which leads to life and the other to destruction.[32] Jesus assumed that his hearers wanted to live in terms of reality and he was concerned to tell them the true nature of reality. From this point of view, the agapeistic way of life follows naturally, via the given structure of the human mind, from belief in the reality of God as *Agape*. However, belief in the reality, love, and power of God issues in the agapeistic way of life (like good fruit from a good tree)[33] only if that belief is taken literally and not merely symbolically. In order to render a distinctive style of life both attractive and rational, it seems that religious beliefs must be regarded as assertions of fact, not merely as imaginative fictions.

## THE LANGUAGE-GAME THEORY

A third influential noncognitive view of religious language derives from the later philosophy of Ludwig Wittgenstein (1889–1951) and has been developed by D. Z. Phillips[34] and others. According to this view, different kinds of language, such as the languages of religion and of science, constitute different "language-games" which are the linguistic aspects of different "forms of life." To participate wholeheartedly in, say, the Christian "form of life" is, among other things, to use distinctively Christian language, which has its own internal criteria determining what is true and false within this universe of

[31]Matthew 7:24f.

[32]Matthew 7:13–14.

[33]Matthew 7:16f.

[34]D. Z. Phillips, *The Concept of Prayer* (London: Routledge and Kegan Paul, 1976, and New York: Seabury Press, Inc., 1981); *Faith and Philosophical Enquiry* (London: Routledge and Kegan Paul, 1970); *Death and Immortality* (London: The Macmillan Company and New York: St. Martin's Press, 1971); *Religion Without Explanation* (Oxford: Basil Blackwell, 1977); and *Belief, Change and Forms of Life* (London: Macmillan and New York: Humanities Press, 1986).

discourse. The internal transactions constituting a given language-game are thus invulnerable to criticism from outside that particular complex of life and language—from which it follows that religious utterances are immune to scientific and other nonreligious comment.

It would, for example, be an authentic piece of traditional Christian discourse to refer to the first man and woman, Adam and Eve, and to their fall from grace in the Garden of Eden, a fall that has made us, along with all their other descendents, guilty before God. According to this Neo-Wittgensteinian theory of religious language, such a way of talking does not clash with the scientific theory that the human race is not descended from a single primal pair, or that the earliest humans did not live in a paradisal state, for science is a different language-game, with its own quite different criteria.

To link religion to mundane facts, whether accessible to common observation or to scientific research, and to require that religious convictions be compatible with those facts, would on this view be profoundly irreligious. Religion is an autonomous form of life with its own language which neither requires support, nor is required to fend off objections, from outside itself. Thus, for example, its affirmation of the goodness of God does not carry any implications about "how the world goes," including the future course of human experience either in or beyond this life. The idea that religion tells us about the actual structure of reality, revealing a larger context of existence than our present earthly life, is on this view a basic mistake. (One has to add, however, that if it is a mistake, it is one that virtually all the great religious founders and teachers seem to have made!)

D. Z. Phillips has applied the view of religion as a distinctive language-game to two themes in particular: prayer and immortality. I shall use the latter to illustrate further this proposal in the philosophy of religion. Whereas the Christian belief in "the life everlasting" has normally been understood as a belief about our destiny after bodily death, and thus as a belief that is factually either true or false and that will, if true, be confirmed in future human experience, Phillips sees it as having no such implications. The soul is the moral personality:

To say of someone "He'd sell his soul for money" is a perfectly natural remark. It in no way entails any philosophical theory about a duality in human nature. The remark is a moral observation about a person, one which expresses the degraded state that person is in. A man's soul, in this context, refers to his integrity, to the complex set of practices and beliefs which acting with integrity would cover for that person. Might not talk about immortality of the soul play a similar role?[35]

[35]Phillips, *Death and Immortality*, p. 43.

Indeed, according to Phillips:

Eternal life is the reality of goodness, that in terms of which human life is to be assessed.…Eternity is not an extension of this present life, but a mode of judging it. Eternity is not *more* life, but this life seen under certain moral and religious modes of thought.…Questions about the immortality of the soul are seen not to be questions concerning the extent of a man's life, and in particular concerning whether that life can extend beyond the grave, but questions concerning the kind of life a man is living.[36]

The positive moral value of this interpretation lies in the release that it prompts from concern with the self and its future:

This renunciation [of the idea of a life to come] is what the believer means by dying to the self. He ceases to see himself as the centre of his world. Death's lesson for the believer is to force him to recognise what all his natural instincts want to resist, namely, that he has no claims on the way things go. Most of all, he is forced to realise that his own life is not a necessity.[37]

On the other hand, critics have pointed out, it does not follow from the fact that we can be (and indeed often are) selfishly concerned about a possible future beyond this life, that there is no such future. In Christian belief, the doctrine of the life to come is grounded, not in human desires, but in the nature of God, who has created us in the divine image and whose love will hold us in being beyond the limits of this present life. Having created men and women with immense potentialities, which only begin to be realized on earth, God will not drop them, half formed, out of existence. As Martin Luther said, "Anyone with whom God speaks, whether in wrath or in mercy, the same is certainly immortal. The Person of God who speaks, and the Word, show that we are creatures with whom God wills to speak, right into eternity, and in an immortal manner."[38]

Indeed, the basic criticism that has been made of the Neo-Wittgensteinian theory of religious language is that it is not (as it professes to be) an account of normal or ordinary religious language use but rather is a proposal for a radical new interpretation of religious utterances. In this new interpretation, religious expressions are systematically deprived of the cosmic implications that they have always been assumed to have. Not only is human immortality reinterpreted as a quality of this present mortal life but, more fundamentally, God is no longer thought of as a reality existing independently of human belief and disbelief. Rather, as Phillips says, "What [the believer] learns is religious

---

[36]*Ibid.*, pp. 48–49.

[37]*Ibid.*, pp. 52–53.

[38]Quoted by Emil Brunner, *Dogmatics,* II, trans. Olive Wyon (Philadelphia: Westminster Press, 1952), p. 69.

language; a language which he participates in along with other believers. What I am suggesting is that to know how to use this language is to know God."[39] Again, "To have the idea of God is to know God."[40] The skeptical possibility for which such a position does not allow is that people have the idea of God, and participate in theistic language, and yet there is no God.

[39]Phillips, *The Concept of Prayer*, p. 50.
[40]*Ibid.*, p. 18.

# CHAPTER 8

# The Problem of Verification

## THE QUESTION OF VERIFIABILITY

In implicit opposition to all noncognitive accounts of religious language, traditional Christian and Jewish faith has always presumed the factual character of its basic assertions. It is, of course, evident even to the most preliminary reflection that theological statements, having a unique subject matter, are not wholly like any other kind of statement. They constitute a special use of language, which it is the task of the philosophy of religion to examine. However, the way in which this language operates within historic Judaism and Christianity is much closer to ordinary factual assertions than to either expressions of aesthetic intuitions or declarations of ethical policies.

In view of this deeply ingrained tendency of traditional theism to use the language of fact, the development within twentieth-century philosophy of a criterion by which to distinguish the factual from the nonfactual is directly relevant to the study of religious language.

Prior to the philosophical movement that began in Vienna, Austria after World War I and became known as Logical Positivism,[1] it was generally assumed that in order to become accepted as true a proposition need only pass one test, a direct examination as to its truth or falsity. The positivists instituted another qualifying examination that a proposition must pass before it can even compete for the Diploma of Truth. This previous examination is concerned

---

[1]For a classic statement of the tenets of Logical Positivism, see A. J. Ayer, *Language, Truth and Logic,* 2nd ed. (London: Victor Gollancz Ltd., 1946, and New York: Dover Publications, Inc., 1946).

with whether or not a proposition is meaningful. "Meaningful" in this context is not a psychological term, as when we speak of "a very meaningful experience" or say of something that "it means a lot to me"; it is a logical term. To say that a proposition has meaning or, more strictly (as became evident in the discussions of the 1930's and 1940's), that it has factual or cognitive meaning, is to say that it is in principle verifiable, or at least "probabilifiable," by reference to human experience. This means, in effect, that its truth or falsity must make some possible experienceable difference. If its truth or falsity makes no difference that could possibly be observed, the proposition is cognitively meaningless; it does not embody a factual assertion.

Suppose, for example, the startling news is announced one morning that overnight the entire physical universe has instantaneously doubled in size and that the speed of light has doubled. At first, this news seems to point to a momentous scientific discovery. All the items composing the universe, including our own bodies, are now twice as big as they were yesterday. But questions concerning the evidence for this report must be raised. How can anyone know that the universe has doubled in size? What observable difference does it make whether this is so or not; what events or appearances are supposed to reveal it? On further reflection, it becomes clear that there *could not* be any evidence for this particular proposition, for if the entire universe has doubled and the speed of light has doubled with it, our measurements have also doubled and we can never know that any change has taken place. If our measuring rod has expanded with the objects to be measured, it cannot measure their expansion. In order adequately to acknowledge the systematic impossibility of testing such a proposition, it seems best to classify it as (cognitively) meaningless. It first seemed to be a genuinely factual assertion, but under scrutiny it proves to lack the basic characteristic of an assertion, namely, that it must make an experienceable difference whether the facts are as alleged or not.

The basic principle—representing a modified version of the original verifiability principle of the logical positivists—that a factual assertion is one whose truth or falsity makes some experienceable difference, has been applied to theological propositions. John Wisdom opened this chapter in the philosophy of religion with his now famous parable of the gardener, which deserves to be quoted here in full:

Two people return to their long-neglected garden and find among the weeds a few of the old plants surprisingly vigorous. One says to the other "It must be that a gardener has been coming and doing something about these plants." Upon inquiry they find that no neighbor has ever seen anyone at work in their garden. The first man says to the other "He must have worked while people slept." The other says, "No, someone would have heard him and besides, anybody who cared about the plants would have kept down these weeds." The first man says, "Look at the way these are arranged. There is purpose and a feeling for beauty here. I believe that someone comes, someone invisible to mortal eyes. I believe that the more carefully we look the more we shall find confirmation of this." They examine the garden ever so carefully and sometimes they come on new things suggesting that a gardener comes and sometimes they come on new things suggesting the contrary and even that a malicious person has been at work. Besides examining the garden carefully they also study what happens to gardens left without attention. Each learns all the other learns about this and about the garden. Consequently, when after all this, one says "I still believe a gardener comes" while the other says "I don't" their different words now reflect no difference as to what they have found in the garden, no difference as to what they would find in the garden if they looked further and no difference about how fast untended gardens fall into disorder. At this stage, in this context, the gardener hypothesis has ceased to be experimental, the difference between one who accepts and one who rejects it is not now a matter of the one expecting something the other does not expect. What is the difference between them? The one says, "A gardener comes unseen and unheard. He is manifested only in his works with which we are all familiar," the other says "There is no gardener" and with this difference in what they say about the gardener goes a difference in how they feel towards the garden, in spite of the fact that neither expects anything of it which the other does not expect.[2]

Wisdom is here suggesting that the theist and the atheist do not disagree about the empirical (experienceable) facts, or about any observations which they anticipate in the future; they are, instead, reacting in different ways to the same set of facts. Understanding them in this way, we can no longer say in any usual sense that one is right and the other wrong. They both really feel about the world in the ways that their words indicate. However, expressions of feelings do not constitute assertions about the world. We would have to speak, instead, of these different feelings being more or less satisfying or valuable: as Santayana said, religions are not true or false but better or worse. According to Wisdom there is no disagreement about the experienceable facts, the settlement of which would determine whether the theist or the atheist is right. In other words, neither of the rival positions is, even in principle, verifiable.

The debate next shifted from the idea of verifiability to the complementary idea of falsifiability. The question was posed whether there is any conceivable event which, if it were to occur, would decisively refute theism? Are there any possible developments of our experience with which theism would be incompatible, or is it equally compatible with whatever may happen? Is anything ruled out by belief in God? Anthony Flew, who has presented the challenge in terms of the Judaic-Christian belief in a loving God, writes as follows:

Now it often seems to people who are not religious as if there was no conceivable event or series of events the occurrence of which would be admitted by sophisticated religious people to be a sufficient reason for conceding "There wasn't a God after all"

[2]"Gods," first published in *Proceedings of the Aristotelian Society* (London, 1944–1945); reprinted here by permission of the editor. Reprinted in *Logic and Language*, I, ed. Antony Flew (Oxford: Basil Blackwell and New York: Mott Ltd., 1951); in John Wisdom, *Philosophy and Psychoanalysis* (Oxford: Basil Blackwell and New York: Mott Ltd., 1953), pp. 154–55; and in John Hick, ed., *Classical and Contemporary Readings in the Philosophy of Religion*, 3rd ed. (Englewood Cliffs, N.J.: Prentice-Hall, Inc., 1989).

or "God does not really love us then." Someone tells us that God loves us as a father loves his children. We are reassured. But then we see a child dying of inoperable cancer of the throat. His earthly father is driven frantic in his efforts to help, but his Heavenly Father reveals no obvious sign of concern. Some qualification is made—God's love is "not a merely human love" or it is "an inscrutable love," perhaps—and we realize that such sufferings are quite compatible with the truth of the assertion that "God loves us as a father (but, of course...)." We are reassured again. But then perhaps we ask: what is this assurance of God's (appropriately qualified) love worth, what is this apparent guarantee really a guarantee against? Just what would have to happen not merely (morally and wrongly) to tempt but also (logically and rightly) to entitle us to say "God does not love us" or even "God does not exist"? I therefore put...the simple central questions, "What would have to occur or to have occurred to constitute for you a disproof of the love of, or of the existence of, God?"[3]

## THE IDEA OF ESCHATOLOGICAL VERIFICATION

In response to these challenges I should like to offer for consideration a constructive suggestion based upon the fact that Christianity includes afterlife beliefs.[4] Here are some preliminary points.

1. The verification of a factual assertion is not the same as a logical demonstration of it. The central core of the idea of verification is the removal of grounds for rational doubt. That a proposition, $p$, is verified means that something happens that makes it clear that $p$ is true. A question is settled, so that there is no longer room for reasonable doubt concerning it. The way in which such grounds are excluded varies, of course, with the subject matter, but the common feature in all cases of verification is the ascertaining of truth by the removal of grounds for rational doubt. Whenever such grounds have been removed, we rightly speak of verification having taken place.

2. Sometimes it is necessary to put oneself in a certain position or to perform some particular operation as a prerequisite of verification. For example, one can only verify "There is a table in the next room" by going into the next room; however, it is to be noted that one is not compelled to do this.

3. Therefore, although "verifiable" normally means "publicly verifiable" (i.e., capable in principle of being verified by anyone), it does not follow that

[3]*New Essays in Philosophical Theology*, eds. Antony Flew and Alasdair Macintyre (London: S.C.M. Press, 1955 and New York: The Macmillan Company, 1956), pp. 98–99.

[4]This suggestion is presented more fully in John Hick, "Theology and Verification," *Theology Today*, XVII, No. 1 (April 1960), reprinted in *The Existence of God*, John Hick, ed. (New York: The Macmillan Company, 1964) and developed in *Faith and Knowledge*, 2nd ed. (Ithaca, N.Y.: Cornell University Press, 1966, and London: Macmillan & Company Ltd., 1967, reissued, Macmillan, 1988). Chap. 8 and in "Eschatological Verification Reconsidered," *Religious Studies*, 13, No. 2 (1977). It is criticized by Paul F. Schmidt in *Religious Knowledge* (New York: The Free Press, 1961), pp. 58–60; by William Blackstone, *The Problem of Religious Knowledge* (Englewood Cliffs, N.J.: Prentice-Hall, Inc., 1963), pp. 112–16; by Kai Nielsen, "Eschatological Verification," *Canadian Journal of Theology*, IX, No. 4 (October 1963), and *Contemporary Critiques of Religion* (London: Macmillan & Company Ltd. and New York: Herder & Herder, Inc., 1971), Chap. 4; by Gregory Kavka, "Eschatological Falsification," and Michael Tooley, "John Hick and the Concept of Eschatological Verification" in *Religious Studies*, 12, No. 2 (1976).

a given verifiable proposition has in fact been or will in fact ever be verified by everyone. The number of people who verify a particular true proposition depends upon all manner of contingent factors.

4. It is possible for a proposition to be in principle verifiable if true but not in principle falsifiable if false. Consider, for example, the proposition that "there are three successive sevens in the decimal determination of $\pi$." So far as the value of $\pi$ has been worked out, it does not contain a series of three sevens; but since the operation can proceed *ad infinitum* it will always be true that a triple seven may occur at a point not yet reached in anyone's calculations. Accordingly, the proposition may one day be verified if it is true but can never be falsified if it is false.

5. The hypothesis of continued conscious existence after bodily death provides another instance of a proposition that is verifiable if true but not falsifiable if false. This hypothesis entails a prediction that one will, after the date of one's bodily death, have conscious experiences, including the experience of remembering that death. This is a prediction that will be verified in one's own experience if it is true but that cannot be falsified if it is false. That is to say, it can be false, but *that* it is false can never be a fact of which anyone has experiential knowledge. This principle does not undermine the meaningfulness of the survival hypothesis, for if its prediction is true, it will be known to be true.

The idea of eschatological verification can now be indicated in the following parable.[5]

Two people are traveling together along a road. One of them believes that it leads to the Celestial City, the other that it leads nowhere; but since this is the only road there is, both must travel it. Neither has been this way before; therefore, neither is able to say what they will find around each corner. During their journey they meet with moments of refreshment and delight, and with moments of hardship and danger. All the time one of them thinks of the journey as a pilgrimage to the Celestial City. She interprets the pleasant parts as encouragements and the obstacles as trials of her purpose and lessons in endurance, prepared by the sovereign of that city and designed to make of her a worthy citizen of the place when at last she arrives. The other, however, believes none of this, and sees their journey as an unavoidable and aimless ramble. Since he has no choice in the matter, he enjoys the good and endures the bad. For him there is no Celestial City to be reached, no all-encompassing purpose ordaining their journey; there is only the road itself and the luck of the road in good weather and in bad.

During the course of the journey, the issue between them is not an experimental one. That is to say, they do not entertain different expectations about

---

[5]This "parable" comes from John Hick, *Faith and Knowledge,* 2nd ed. (reissued London: Macmillan, 1988), pp. 177–78.

the coming details of the road, but only about its ultimate destination. Yet, when they turn the last corner, it will be apparent that one of them has been right all the time and the other wrong. Thus, although the issue between them has not been experimental, it has nevertheless been a real issue. They have not merely felt differently about the road, for one was feeling appropriately and the other inappropriately in relation to the actual state of affairs. Their opposed interpretations of the situation have constituted genuinely rival assertions, whose assertion-status has the peculiar characteristic of being guaranteed retrospectively by a future crux.

This parable, like all parables, has its limitations. It is designed to make only one point: that Judaic-Christian theism postulates an ultimate unambiguous existence *in patria*, as well as our present ambiguous existence *in via*. There is a state of having arrived as well as a state of journeying, an eternal heavenly life as well as an earthly pilgrimage. The alleged future experience cannot, of course, be appealed to as evidence for theism as a present interpretation of our experience, but it does apparently suffice to render the choice between theism and atheism a real and not an empty or merely verbal choice.

The universe as envisaged by the theist, then, differs as a totality from the universe as envisaged by the atheist. However, from our present standpoint within the universe, this difference does not involve a difference in the objective content of each or even any of its passing moments. The theist and the atheist do not (or need not) expect different events to occur in the successive details of the temporal process. They do not (or need not) entertain divergent expectations of the course of history viewed from within. However, the theist does and the atheist does not expect that when history is completed, it will be seen to have led to a particular end state and to have fulfilled a specific purpose, namely, that of creating "children of God."

## SOME DIFFICULTIES AND COMPLICATIONS

Even if it were granted (as of course many philosophers would not be willing to grant) that it makes sense to speak of continued personal existence after death, an experience of survival would not necessarily serve to verify theism. It might be taken as just a surprising natural fact. The deceased atheist able to remember life on earth might find that the universe has turned out to be more complex, and perhaps more to be approved of, then he or she had realized. However, the mere fact of survival, with a new body in a new environment, would not by itself demonstrate to such a person the reality of God. The life to come might turn out to be as religiously ambiguous as this present life. It might still be quite unclear whether or not there is a God.

Should appeal be made at this point to the traditional doctrine, which figures especially in Catholic and mystical theology, of the Beatific Vision of

God? The difficulty is to attach any precise meaning to this phrase.[6] If it is to be more than a poetic metaphor, it signifies that embodied beings see the visible figure of the deity. But to speak in this way would be to think of God as an object in space. If we are to follow the implications of the deeper insights of the Western tradition, we shall have to think instead of an experienced *situation* that points unambiguously to the reality of God. The consciousness of God will still be, formally, a matter of faith in that it will continue to involve an activity of interpretation. But the data to be interpreted, instead of being bafflingly ambiguous, will at all points confirm religious faith. We are thus postulating a situation that contrasts in an important respect with our present situation. Our present experience of this world in some ways seems to support and in other ways to contradict a religious faith. Some events suggest the reality of an unseen and benevolent intelligence, and others suggest that no such intelligence can be at work. Our environment is thus religiously ambiguous. In order for us to be aware of this fact, we must already have some idea, however vague, of what it would be for a world to be not ambiguous but on the contrary wholly evidential of God. Is it possible to draw out this presupposed idea of a religiously unambiguous situation?

Although it is difficult to say what future experiences would verify theism in general, it is less difficult to say what would verify the more specific claims of such a religion as Christianity, with its own built-in eschatological beliefs. The system of ideas that surrounds the Christian concept of God, and in the light of which that concept has to be understood, includes expectations concerning the final fulfillment of God's purpose for humanity in the "Kingdom of God." The experience that would verify Christian belief in God is the experience of participating in that eventual fulfillment. According to the New Testament, the general nature of God's purpose for human life is the creation of "children of God" who shall participate in eternal life. One can say this much without professing advance knowledge of the concrete forms of such a fulfillment. The situation is analogous to that of a small child looking forward to adult life and then, having grown to adulthood, looking back upon childhood. The child possesses and can use correctly the concept of "being grown-up," although, as a child, one does not yet know what it is like to be grown-up. When one reaches adulthood, one is, nevertheless, able to know that one has reached it, for one's understanding of adult maturity grows as one matures. Something analogous may be supposed to happen in the case of the fulfillment of the divine purpose for human life. That fulfillment may be as far removed from our present condition as is mature adulthood from the mind of a little child. Indeed, it may be much further removed; but we already possess some notion of it (given in the person of Christ), and as we move toward it our concept will thereby become more adequate. If and when we finally reach that fulfillment, the problem of recognizing it will have disappeared in the process.

---

[6]Aquinas attempts to make the idea intelligible in his *Summa contra Gentiles*, Book III, Chap. 51.

## "EXISTS," "FACT," AND "REAL"

Can we, then, properly ask whether God "exists"? If we do so, what precisely are we asking? Does "exist" have a single meaning, so that one can ask, in the same sense, "Do flying fish exist; does the square root of minus one exist; does the Freudian superego exist; does God exist?" It seems clear that we are asking very different kinds of questions in these different cases. To ask whether flying fish exist is to ask whether a certain form of organic life is to be found in the oceans of the world. On the other hand, to ask whether the square root of minus one exists is not to ask whether there is a certain kind of material object somewhere, but is to pose a question about the conventions of mathematics. To ask whether the superego exists is to ask whether one accepts the Freudian picture of the structure of the psyche; and this is a decision to which a great variety of considerations may be relevant. To ask whether God exists is to ask—what? Not, certainly, whether there is a particular physical object. Is it (as in the mathematical case) to inquire about linguistic conventions? Or is it (as in the psychological case) to inquire about a great mass of varied considerations—perhaps even the character of our experience as a whole? What, in short, does it mean to affirm that God exists?

It would be no answer to this question to refer to the idea of divine aseity[7] and to say that the difference between the ways in which God and other realities exist is that God exists necessarily and everything else contingently. We still want to know what it is that God is doing or undergoing in existing necessarily rather than contingently. (We do not learn what electricity is by being told that some electrical circuits have an alternating and others a direct current; likewise, we do not learn what it is to exist by being told that some things exist necessarily and others contingently.)

For those who adopt one or another of the various noncognitive accounts of religious language, there is no problem concerning the sense in which God "exists." If they use the expression "God exists" at all, they understand it as referring obliquely to the speaker's own feelings or attitudes or moral commitments, or to the character of the empirical world. But what account of "God exists" can be given by the traditional theist, who holds that God exists as the Creator and the ultimate Ruler of the universe?

The same question can be posed in terms of the idea of "fact." The theist claims that the existence of God is a question of fact rather than merely of definition or of linguistic usage. The theist also uses the term "real," and claims that God is real or a reality. But what do these words mean in this context? The problem is essentially the same whether one employs "exist," "fact," or "real."

A suggestion that coheres with the idea of eschatological verification is that the common core to the concepts of "existence," "fact," and "reality" is the

[7]For an explanation of this term, see p. 8.

idea of "making a difference." To say that $x$ exists or is real, that it is a fact that there is an $x$, is to claim that the character of the universe differs in some specific way from the character that an $x$-less universe would have. The nature of this difference will naturally depend upon the character of the $x$ in question, and the meaning of "God exists" will be indicated by spelling out the past, present, and future difference which God's existence is alleged to make within human experience.

# CHAPTER 9

# The Conflicting Truth Claims of Different Religions

## MANY FAITHS, ALL CLAIMING TO BE TRUE

Until comparatively recently each of the different religions of the world had developed in substantial ignorance of the others. There have been, it is true, great movements of expansion which have brought two faiths into contact: above all, the expansion of Buddhism during the last three centuries B.C.E. and the early centuries of the Christian era, carrying its message throughout India and Southeast Asia and into China, Tibet, and Japan, and then, the resurgence of the Hindu religion at the expense of Buddhism, with the result that today Buddhism is rarely to be found on the Indian subcontinent; next, the first Christian expansion into the Roman Empire; then the expansion of Islam in the seventh and eighth centuries C.E. into the Middle East, Europe, and later India; and finally, the second expansion of Christianity in the missionary movement of the nineteenth century. These interactions, however, in the cases of Christianity and Islam, were conflicts rather than dialogues; they did not engender any deep or sympathetic understanding of one faith by the adherents of another. It is only during the last hundred years or so that the scholarly study of world religions has made possible an accurate appreciation of the faiths of other people and so has brought home to an increasing number of us the problem of the conflicting truth claims made by different religious traditions. This issue now emerges as a major topic demanding a prominent place on the agenda of the philosopher of religion.

The problem can be posed very concretely in this way. If I had been born in India, I would probably be a Hindu; if in Egypt, probably a Muslim; if in Sri

Lanka, probably a Buddhist; but I was born in England and am, predictably, a Christian. (Of course, a different "I" would have developed in each case.) These different religions seem to say different and incompatible things about the nature of ultimate reality, about the modes of divine activity, and about the nature and destiny of the human race. Is the divine nature personal or nonpersonal? Does deity become incarnate in the world? Are human beings reborn again and again on earth? Is the empirical self the real self, destined for eternal life in fellowship with God, or is it only a temporary and illusory manifestation of an eternal higher self? Is the Bible, or the Qur'an, or the Bhagavad Gita the Word of God? If what Christianity says in answer to such questions is true, must not what Hinduism says be to a large extent false? If what Buddhism says is true, must not what Islam says be largely false?

The skeptical thrust of these questions goes very deep; for it is a short step from the thought that the different religions cannot all be true, although they each claim to be, to the thought that in all probability none of them is true. Thus Hume laid down the principle "that, in matters of religion, whatever is different is contrary; and that it is impossible the religions of ancient Rome, of Turkey, of Siam, and of China should, all of them, be established on any solid foundation." Accordingly, regarding miracles as evidence for the truth of a particular faith, "Every miracle, therefore, pretended to have been wrought in any of these religions (and all of them abound in miracles), as its direct scope is to establish the particular religion to which it is attributed; so has it the same force, though more indirectly, to overthrow every other system."[1] By the same reasoning, any ground for believing a particular religion to be true must operate as a ground for believing every other religion to be false; accordingly, for any particular religion there will always be far more reason for believing it to be false than for believing it to be true. This is the skeptical argument that arises from the conflicting truth claims of the various world faiths.

## CRITIQUE OF THE CONCEPT OF "A RELIGION"

In his important book *The Meaning and End of Religion*,[2] Wilfred Cantwell Smith challenges the familiar concept of "a religion," upon which much of the traditional problem of conflicting religious truth claims rests. He emphasizes that what we call a religion—an empirical entity that can be traced historically and mapped geographically—is a human phenomenon. Christianity, Hinduism, Judaism, Buddhism, Islam, and so on are human creations whose history is part of the wider history of human culture. Cantwell Smith traces the

[1]David Hume, *An Enquiry Concerning Human Understanding*, 1748, ed. L. A. Selby-Bigge (Oxford: Clarendon Press, 1936), para. 95, p. 121.
[2]Wilfred Cantwell Smith, *The Meaning and End of Religion*, 1962 (New York: Harper & Row and London: Sheldon Press, 1978).

development of the concept of a religion as a clear and bounded historical phenomenon and shows that the notion, far from being universal and self-evident, is a distinctively western invention which has been exported to the rest of the world. "It is," he says, summarizing the outcome of his detailed historical argument, "a surprisingly modern aberration for anyone to think that Christianity is true or that Islam is—since the Enlightenment, basically, when Europe began to postulate religions as intellectualistic systems, patterns of doctrine, so that they could for the first time be labeled 'Christianity' and 'Buddhism,' and could be called true or false."[3] The names by which we know the various "religions" today were in fact (with the exception of "Islam") invented in the eighteenth century, and before they were imposed by the influence of the West upon the peoples of the world no one had thought of himself or herself as belonging to one of a set of competing systems of belief concerning which it is possible to ask, "Which of these systems is the true one?" This notion of religions as mutually exclusive entities with their own characteristics and histories—although it now tends to operate as a habitual category of our thinking—may well be an example of the illicit reification, the turning of good adjectives into bad substantives, to which the western mind is prone and against which contemporary philosophy has warned us. In this case a powerful but distorting conceptuality has helped to create phenomena answering to it, namely the religions of the world seeing themselves and each other as rival ideological communities.

Perhaps, however, instead of thinking of religion as existing in mutually exclusive systems, we should see the religious life of humanity as a dynamic continuum within which certain major disturbances have from time to time set up new fields of force, of greater or lesser power, displaying complex relationships of attraction and repulsion, absorption, resistance, and reinforcement. These major disturbances are the great creative religious moments of human history from which the distinguishable religious traditions have stemmed. Theologically, such moments are seen as intersections of divine grace, divine initiative, divine truth, with human faith, human response, human enlightenment. They have made their impact upon the stream of human life so as to affect the development of cultures; and what we call Christianity, Islam, Hinduism, Buddhism, are among the resulting historical-cultural phenomena. It is clear, for example, that Christianity has developed through a complex interaction between religious and nonreligious factors. Christian ideas have been formed within the intellectual framework provided by Greek philosophy; the Christian church was molded as an institution by the Roman Empire and its system of laws; the Catholic mind reflects something of Latin Mediterranean and the Protestant mind something of northern Germanic culture, and so on. It is not hard to appreciate the connections between historical Christianity and the continuing life of humanity in the

[3]Wilfred Cantwell Smith, *Questions of Religious Truth* (London: Victor Gollancz Ltd., 1967), p. 73.

western hemisphere, and of course the same is true, in their own ways, of all the other religions of the world.

This means that it is not appropriate to speak of a religion as being true or false, any more than it is to speak of a civilization as being true or false. For the religions, in the sense of distinguishable religiocultural streams within human history, are expressions of the diversities of human types and temperaments and thought forms. The same differences between the eastern and western mentality that are revealed in characteristically different conceptual and linguistic, social, political, and artistic forms presumably also underlie the contrasts between eastern and western religion.

In *The Meaning and End of Religion* Cantwell Smith examines the development from the original religious event or idea—whether it be the insight of the Buddha, the life of Christ, or the career of Mohammed—to a religion in the sense of a vast living organism with its own credal backbone and its institutional skin. He shows in each case that this development stands in a questionable relationship to that original event or idea. Religions as institutions, with the theological doctrines and the codes of behavior that form their boundaries, did not come about because the religious reality required this, but because such a development was historically inevitable in the days of undeveloped communication between the different cultural groups. Now that the world has become a communicational unity, we are moving into a new situation in which it becomes both possible and appropriate for religious thinking to transcend these cultural-historical boundaries. But what form might such new thinking take, and how would it affect the problem of conflicting truth claims?

## TOWARD A POSSIBLE SOLUTION

To see the historical inevitability of the plurality of religions in the past and its noninevitability in the future, we must note the broad course that has been taken by the religious life of humanity. Humanity has been described as a naturally religious animal, displaying an innate tendency to experience the environment as being religiously as well as naturally significant and to feel required to live in it as such. This tendency is universally expressed in the cultures of early peoples, with their belief in sacred objects, endowed with *mana*, and in a multitude of spirits needing to be carefully propitiated. The divine reality is here apprehended as a plurality of quasi-animal forces. The next stage seems to have come with the coalescence of tribes into larger groups. The tribal gods were then ranked in hierarchies (some being lost by amalgamation in the process) dominated, in the Middle East, by great national gods such as the Sumerian Ishtar, Amon of Thebes, Jahweh of Israel, Marduk of Babylon, the Greek Zeus, and in India by the Vedic high gods such as Dyaus (the sky god), Varuna (god of heaven), and Agni (the fire god). The world of such national and nature gods, often martial and cruel and sometimes requiring human sacrifices, reflected the state of humanity's awareness of the divine at the dawn of documentary history, some three thousand years ago.

So far, the whole development can be described as the growth of natural religion. That is to say, primal spirit worship expressing fear of the unknown forces of nature, and later the worship of regional deities—depicting either aspects of nature (sun, sky, etc.) or the collective personality of a nation—represent the extent of humanity's religious life prior to any special intrusions of divine revelation or illumination.

But sometime after 1000 B.C.E. a golden age of religious creativity, named by Jaspers the Axial Period,[4] dawned. This consisted of a series of revelatory experiences occurring in different parts of the world that deepened and purified people's conceptions of the divine, and that religious faith can only attribute to the pressure of the divine reality upon the human spirit. To quote A. C. Bouquet, "It is a commonplace with specialists in the history of religion that somewhere within the region of 800 B.C. there passed over the populations of this planet a stirring of the mind, which, while it left large tracts of humanity comparatively uninfluenced, produced in a number of different spots on the earth's surface prophetic individuals who created a series of new starting points for human living and thinking."[5] At the threshold of this period some of the great Hebrew prophets appeared (Elijah in the ninth century; Amos, Hosea, and the first Isaiah in the eighth century; and then Jeremiah in the seventh), declaring that they had heard the word of the Lord claiming their obedience and demanding a new level of righteousness and justice in the life of Israel. During the next five centuries, between about 800 and 300 B.C.E., the prophet Zoroaster appeared in Persia; Greece produced Pythagoras, and then Socrates and Plato, and Aristotle; in China there was Confucius, and the author or authors of the Taoist scriptures; and in India this creative period saw the formation of the Upanishads and the lives of Gotama the Buddha, and Mahavira, founder of the Jain religion, and around the end of this period, the writing of the *Bhagavad Gita*. Even Christianity, beginning later, and then Islam, both have their roots in the Hebrew religion of the Axial Age and both can hardly be understood except in relation to it.

It is important to observe the situation within which all these revelatory moments occurred. Communication between the different groups of humanity was then so limited that for all practical purposes human beings inhabited a series of different worlds. For the most part people living in China, in India, in Arabia, in Persia, were unaware of the others' existence. There was thus, inevitably, a multiplicity of local religions that were also local civilizations.

---

[4]Karl Jaspers, *The Origin and Goal of History,* 1949 (New Haven: Yale University Press, 1953), Chap. 1.

[5]A. C. Bouquet, *Comparative Religion* (Harmondsworth, Middlesex: Penguin Books Ltd., 1941), pp. 77–78.

Accordingly the great creative moments of revelation and illumination occurred separately within the different cultures and influenced their development, giving them the coherence and confidence to expand into larger units,
thus producing the vast religiocultural entities that we now call the world
religions. So it is that until recently the different streams of religious experience and belief have flowed through different cultures, each forming and
being formed by its own separate environment. There has, of course, been
contact between different religions at certain points in history, and an influence—sometimes an important influence—of one upon another; nevertheless,
the broad picture is one of religions developing separately within their different historical and cultural settings.

In addition to noting these historical circumstances, we need to make use
of the important distinction between, on the one hand, human encounters
with the divine reality in the various forms of religious experience, and on the
other hand, theological theories or doctrines that men and women have
developed to conceptualize the meaning of these encounters. These two
components of religion, although distinguishable, are not separable. It is as
hard to say which came first, as in the celebrated case of the hen and the egg;
they continually react upon one another in a joint process of development,
experience providing the ground of our beliefs, but these in turn influencing
the forms taken by our experience. The different religions are different streams
of religious experience, each having started at a different point within human
history and each having formed its own conceptual self-consciousness within
a different cultural milieu.

In the light of this it is possible to consider the hypothesis that the great
religions are all, at their experiential roots, in contact with the same ultimate
divine reality but that their differing experiences of that reality, interacting
over the centuries with the differing thought forms of differing cultures, have
led to increasing differentiation and contrasting elaboration—so that Hinduism, for example, is a very different phenomenon from Christianity, and very
different ways of experiencing and conceiving the divine occur within them.
However, in the "one world" of today the religious traditions are consciously
interacting with each other in mutual observation and dialogue, and it is
possible that their future developments may move on gradually converging
courses. During the next centuries each group will presumably continue to
change, and it may be that they will grow closer together, so that one day such
names as "Christianity," "Buddhism," "Islam," and "Hinduism" will no
longer adequately describe the then current configurations of religious experience and belief. I am not thinking here of the extinction of human religious-
ness in a universal secularization. That is of course a possible future, and
indeed many think it the most likely future to come about. But if the human
creature is an indelibly religious animal, he or she will always, even amidst
secularization, experience a sense of the transcendent that both troubles and
uplifts. The future I am envisaging is accordingly one in which the presently

existing religions will constitute the past history of different emphases and variations, which will then be more like, for example, the different denominations of Christianity in North America or Europe today than like radically exclusive totalities.

If the nature of religion, and the history of religion, is indeed such that a development of this kind begins to take place during the twenty-first century, what would this imply concerning the problem of the conflicting truth claims of the different religions?

We may distinguish three aspects of this question: differences in modes of experiencing the divine reality; differences of philosophical and theological theory concerning that reality or concerning the implications of religious experience; and differences in the key or revelatory experiences that unify a stream of religious life.

The most prominent example of the first kind of difference is probably that between the experience of the divine as personal and as nonpersonal. In Judaism, Christianity, Islam, and the theistic strand of Hinduism, the Ultimate is apprehended as personal goodness, will, and purpose under the different names of Jahweh, God, Allah, Vishnu, Shiva. On the other hand, in Hinduism as interpreted by the Advaita Vedānta school, and in Theravada Buddhism, ultimate reality is apprehended as nonpersonal. Mahayana Buddhism is a more complex tradition, including both nontheistic Zen and quasi-theistic Pure Land Buddhism. There is, perhaps, in principle no difficulty in holding that these personal and nonpersonal experiences of the Ultimate can be understood as complementary rather than as incompatible. For if, as every profound form of religion has affirmed, the Ultimate Reality is infinite and exceeds the scope of our finite human categories, that reality may be both personal Lord and nonpersonal Ground of being. At any rate, there is a program for thought in the exploration of what Aurobindo called "the logic of the infinite"[6] and the question of the extent to which predicates that are incompatible when attributed to a finite reality may no longer be incompatible when referred to infinite reality.

The second type of difference is in philosophical and theological theory or doctrine. Such differences, and indeed conflicts, are not merely apparent, but they are part of the still developing history of human thought; it may be that in time they will be transcended, for they belong to the historical, culturally conditioned aspect of religion, which is subject to change. When one considers, for example, the immense changes that have come about within Christian thought during the last hundred years, in response to the development of modern biblical scholarship and the modern physical and biological sciences, one can set no limit to the further developments that may take place in the future. A book of contemporary Christian theology (post-Darwin, post-Ein-

[6]Sri Aurobindo, *The Life Divine* (Pondicherry: Sri Aurobindo Ashram, 1949, and N.Y.: Matagiri Sri Aurobindo Center, Inc., 1980), Book II, Chap. 2.

stein, post-Freud), using modern biblical criticism and taking for granted a considerable demythologization of the New Testament world view, would have been quite unrecognizable as Christian theology two centuries ago. Comparable responses to modern science are yet to occur in many of the other religions of the world, but they must inevitably come, sooner or later. When all the main religious traditions have been through their own encounter with modern science, they will probably have undergone as considerable an internal development as has Christianity. In addition, there will be an increasing influence of each faith upon every other as they meet and interact more freely within the "one world" of today. In the light of all this, the future that I have speculatively projected does not seem impossible.

However, it is the third kind of difference that constitutes the largest difficulty in the way of religious agreement. Each religion has its holy founder or scripture, or both, in which the divine reality has been revealed—the Vedas, the Torah, the Buddha, Christ and the Bible, the Qur'an. Wherever the Holy is revealed, it claims an absolute response of faith and worship, which thus seems incompatible with a like response to any other claimed disclosure of the Holy. Within Christianity, for example, this absoluteness and exclusiveness of response has been strongly developed in the doctrine that Christ was uniquely divine, the only Son of God, of one substance with the Father, the only mediator between God and man. But this traditional doctrine, formed in an age of substantial ignorance of the wider religious life of humanity, gives rise today to an acute tension. On the one hand, Christianity traditionally teaches that God is the Creator and Lord of all humanity and seeks humanity's final good and salvation; and on the other hand that only by responding in faith to God in Christ can we be saved. This means that infinite love has ordained that human beings can be saved only in a way that in fact excludes the large majority of them; for the greater part of all the human beings who have been born have lived either before Christ or outside the borders of Christendom. In an attempt to meet this glaring paradox, Christian theology has developed a doctrine according to which those outside the circle of Christian faith may nevertheless be saved. For example, the Second Vatican Council of the Roman Catholic Church, 1963–1965, declared that "Those who through no fault of their own are still ignorant of the Gospel of Christ and of his Church yet sincerely seek God and, with the help of divine grace, strive to do his will as known to them through the voice of their conscience, those men can attain to eternal salvation."[7] This represents a real movement in response to a real problem; nevertheless it is only an epicycle of theory, complicating the existing dogmatic system rather than going to the heart of the problem. The epicycle is designed to cover theists ("those who sincerely seek God") who have had no contact with the Christian gospel. But what of the nontheistic Buddhists and nontheistic Hindus? And what of those Muslims, Jews, Bud-

---

[7]*Dogmatic Constitution on the Church*, Art. 16.

dhists, Hindus, Jains, Parsees, etc., both theists and nontheists, who have heard the Christian gospel but have preferred to adhere to the faith of their fathers?

Thus it seems that if the tension at the heart of the traditional Christian attitude to non-Christian faiths is to be resolved, Christian thinkers must give even more radical attention to the problem than they have as yet done. It is, however, not within the scope of this book to suggest a plan for the reconstruction of Christian or other religious doctrines.

## A PHILOSOPHICAL FRAMEWORK FOR RELIGIOUS PLURALISM

Among the great religious traditions, and particularly within their more mystical strands, a distinction is widely recognized between the Real or Ultimate or Divine *an sich* (in him/her/its-self) and the Real as conceptualized and experienced by human beings. The widespread assumption is that the Ultimate Reality is infinite and as such exceeds the grasp of human thought and language, so that the describable and experienceable objects of worship and contemplation are not the Ultimate in its limitless reality but the Ultimate in its relationship to finite perceivers. One form of this distinction is that between *nirguna* Brahman, Brahman without attributes, beyond the scope of human thought, and *saguna* Brahman, Brahman with attributes, encountered within human experience as Ishvara, the personal creator and governor of the universe. In the West the Christian mystic Meister Eckhart drew a parallel distinction between the Godhead (*Deitas*) and God (*Deus*). The Taoist scripture, the *Tao Te Ching*, begins by affirming that "The Tao that can be expressed is not the eternal Tao." The Jewish Kabbalist mystics distinguished between En Soph, the absolute divine reality beyond all human description, and the God of the Bible; and among the Muslim Sufis, Al Haqq, the Real, seems to be a similar concept to En Soph, as the abyss of Godhead underlying the self-revealing Allah. More recently Paul Tillich has spoken of "the God above the God of theism";[8] and Gordon Kaufman has recently distinguished between the "real God" and the "available God."[9] These all seem to be somewhat similar (though not identical) distinctions. If we suppose that the Real is one, but that our human perceptions of the Real are plural and various, we have a basis for the hypothesis that the different streams of religious experience represent diverse awarenesses of the same limitless transcendent reality, which is perceived in characteristically different ways by different human mentalities, forming and formed by different cultural histories.

Immanuel Kant has provided (without intending to do so) a philosophical framework within which such a hypothesis can be developed. He distin-

[8]Paul Tillich, *The Courage to Be* (New Haven: Yale University Press, 1952), p. 190.
[9]Gordon Kaufman, *God the Problem* (Cambridge, Mass.: Harvard University Press, 1972), p. 86.

guished between the world as it is *an sich*, which he called the noumenal world, and the world as it appears to human consciousness, which he called the phenomenal world. His writings can be interpreted in various ways, but according to one interpretation the phenomenal world *is* the noumenal world as humanly experienced. The innumerable diverse sensory clues are brought together in human consciousness, according to Kant, by means of a system of relational concepts or categories (such as "thing" and "cause") in terms of which we are aware of our environment. Thus our environment as we perceive it is a joint product of the world itself and the selecting, interpreting, and unifying activity of the perceiver. Kant was concerned mainly with the psychological contribution to our awareness of the world, but the basic principle can also be seen at work on the physiological level. Our sensory equipment is capable of responding to only a minute proportion of the full range of sound and electromagnetic waves—light, radio, infrared, ultraviolet, X, and gamma—which are impinging upon us all the time. Consequently, the world as we experience it represents a particular selection—a distinctively human selection—from the immense complexity and richness of the world as it is *an sich*. We experience at a certain macro/micro level. What we experience and use as the solid, enduring table would be, to a micro-observer, a swirling universe of discharging energy, consisting of electrons, neutrons, and quarks in continuous rapid activity. We perceive the world as it appears specifically to beings with our particular physical and psychological equipment. Indeed, the way the world *appears* to us is the way the world *is for us* as we inhabit and interact with it. As Thomas Aquinas said long ago, "The thing known is in the knower according to the mode of the knower."[10]

Is it possible to adopt the broad Kantian distinction between the world as it is in itself and the world as it appears to us with our particular cognitive machinery, and apply it to the relation between the Ultimate Reality and our different human awarenesses of that Reality? If so, we shall think in terms of a single divine noumenon and many diverse divine phenomena. We may form the hypothesis that the Real *an sich* is experienced by human beings in terms of one of two basic religious concepts. One is the concept of God, or of the Real experienced as personal, which presides over the theistic forms of religion. The other is the concept of the Absolute, or of the Real experienced as nonpersonal, which presides over the various nontheistic forms of religion. Each of these basic concepts is, however, made more concrete (in Kantian terminology, schematized) as a range of particular images of God or particular concepts of the Absolute. These images of God are formed within the different religious histories. Thus the Jahweh of the Hebrew Scriptures exists in interaction with the Jewish people. He is a part of their history and they are a part of his; he cannot be abstracted from this particular concrete historical nexus. On the other hand, Krishna is a quite different divine figure, existing in

[10]*Summa Theologica*, II/II, Q.1, Art. 2.

relation to a different faith-community with its own different and distinctive religious ethos. Given the basic hypothesis of the reality of the Divine, we may say that Jahweh and Krishna (and likewise, Shiva, and Allah, and the Father of Jesus Christ) are different *personae* in terms of which the divine Reality is experienced and thought within different streams of religious life. These different *personae* are thus partly projections of the divine Reality into human consciousness, and partly projections of the human consciousness itself as it has been formed by particular historical cultures. From the human end they are our different images of God; from the divine end they are God's *personae* in relation to the different human histories of faith.

A similar account will then have to be given of the forms of nonpersonal Absolute, or *impersonae*, experienced within the different strands of nontheistic religion—Brahman, Nirvana, Sunyata, the Dharma, the Dharmakaya, the Tao. Here, according to our hypothesis, the same limitless Ultimate Reality is being experienced and thought through different forms of the concept of the Real as nonpersonal.

It is characteristic of the more mystical forms of awareness of the Real that they seem to be direct, and not mediated—or therefore distorted—by the perceptual machinery of the human mind. However, our hypothesis will have to hold that even the apparently direct and unmediated awareness of the Real in the Hindu *moksha*, in the Buddhist *satori*, and in the unitive mysticism of the West, is still the conscious experience of a human subject and as such is influenced by the interpretative set of the cognizing mind. All human beings have been influenced by the culture of which they are a part and have received, or have developed in their appropriation of it, certain deep interpretative tendencies which help to form their experience and are thus continually confirmed within it. We see evidence of such deep "sets" at work when we observe that mystics formed by Hindu, Buddhist, Christian, Muslim, and Jewish religious cultures report distinctively different forms of experience. Thus, far from it being the case that they all undergo an identical experience but report it in different religious languages, it seems more probable that they undergo characteristically different unitive experiences (even though with important common features), the differences being due to the conceptual frameworks and meditational disciplines supplied by the religious traditions in which they participate.[11]

Thus it is a possible, and indeed an attractive, hypothesis—as an alternative to total skepticism—that the great religious traditions of the world represent different human perceptions of and response to the same infinite divine Reality.

[11]Concerning this understanding of mysticism, see further Steven Katz, ed., *Mysticism and Philosophical Analysis* (New York: Oxford University Press, 1978).

# CHAPTER 10

# Human Destiny: Immortality and Resurrection

---

## THE IMMORTALITY OF THE SOUL

Some kind of distinction between physical body and immaterial or semimaterial soul seems to be as old as human culture; the existence of such a distinction is indicated by the manner of burial of the earliest human skeletons yet discovered. Anthropologists offer various conjectures about the origin of the distinction: perhaps it was first suggested by memories of dead persons, by dreams of them, by the sight of reflections of oneself in water and on other bright surfaces, or by meditation upon the significance of religious rites which grew up spontaneously in face of the fact of death.

It was Plato (428/7–348/7 B.C.), the philosopher who has most deeply and lastingly influenced western culture, who systematically developed the body–mind dichotomy and first attempted to prove the immortality of the soul.[1]

Plato argues that although the body belongs to the sensible world[2] and shares its changing and impermanent nature, the intellect is related to the unchanging realities of which we are aware when we think not of particular good things but of Goodness itself, not of specific just acts but of Justice itself, and of the other "universals" or eternal Ideas by participation in which physical things and events have their own specific characteristics. Being related to this higher and abiding realm rather than to the evanescent world of sense, the soul is immortal. Hence, one who devotes one's life to the

---

[1] *Phaedo.*

[2] The world known to us through our physical senses.

contemplation of eternal realities rather than to the gratification of the fleeting desires of the body will find at death that whereas the body turns to dust, one's soul gravitates to the realm of the unchanging, there to live forever. Plato painted an awe-inspiring picture, of haunting beauty and persuasiveness, which has moved and elevated the minds of men and women in many different centuries and lands. Nevertheless, it is not today (as it was during the first centuries of the Christian era) the common philosophy of the West; and a demonstration of immortality which presupposes Plato's metaphysical system cannot claim to constitute a proof for a twentieth-century person.

Plato used the further argument that the only things that can suffer destruction are those which are composite, since to destroy something means to disintegrate it into its constituent parts. All material bodies are composite; the soul, however, is simple and therefore imperishable. This argument was adopted by Aquinas and became standard in Roman Catholic theology, as in the following passage from the Catholic philosopher Jacques Maritain:

A spiritual soul cannot be corrupted, since it possesses no matter; it cannot be disintegrated, since it has no substantial parts; it cannot lose its individual unity, since it is self-subsisting, nor its internal energy, since it contains within itself all the sources of its energies. The human soul cannot die. Once it exists, it cannot disappear; it will necessarily exist for ever, endure without end. Thus, philosophic reason, put to work by a great metaphysician like Thomas Aquinas, is able to prove the immortality of the human soul in a demonstrative manner.[3]

This type of reasoning has been criticized on several grounds. Kant pointed out that although it is true that a simple substance cannot disintegrate, consciousness may nevertheless cease to exist through the diminution of its intensity to zero.[4] Modern psychology has also questioned the basic premise that the mind is a simple entity. It seems instead to be a structure of only relative unity, normally fairly stable and tightly integrated but capable under stress of various degrees of division and dissolution. This comment from psychology makes it clear that the assumption that the soul is a simple substance is not an empirical observation but a metaphysical theory. As such, it cannot provide the basis for a general proof of immortality.

The body–soul distinction, first formulated as a philosophical doctrine in ancient Greece, was baptized into Christianity, ran through the medieval period, and entered the modern world with the public status of a self-evident truth when it was redefined in the seventeenth century by Descartes. Since World War II, however, the Cartesian mind–matter dualism, having been

[3]Jacques Maritain, *The Range of Reason* (London: Geoffrey Bles Ltd. and New York: Charles Scribner's Sons, 1953), p. 60.

[4]Kant, *Critique of Pure Reason, Transcendental Dialectic,* "Refutation of Mendelssohn's Proof of the Permanence of the Soul."

taken for granted for many centuries, has been strongly criticized.[5] It is argued that the words that describe mental characteristics and operations—such as "intelligent," "thoughtful," "carefree," "happy," "calculating," and the like—apply in practice to types of human behavior and to behavioral dispositions. They refer to the empirical individual, the observable human being who is born and grows and acts and feels and dies, and not to the shadowy proceedings of a mysterious "ghost in the machine." An individual is thus very much what he or she appears to be—a creature of flesh and blood, who behaves and is capable of behaving in a characteristic range of ways—rather than a non-physical soul incomprehensibly interacting with a physical body.

As a result of this development, much mid-twentieth-century philosophy has come to see the human being as in the biblical writings, not as an eternal soul temporarily attached to a mortal body, but as a form of finite, mortal, psychophysical life. Thus, the Old Testament scholar J. Pedersen said of the Hebrews that for them "the body is the soul in its outward form."[6] This way of thinking has led to quite a different conception of death from that found in Plato and the Neoplatonic strand in European thought.

## THE RE-CREATION OF THE PSYCHOPHYSICAL PERSON

Only toward the end of the Old Testament period did afterlife beliefs come to have any real importance within Judaism. Previously, Hebrew religious insight had focused so fully upon God's covenant with the nation, as an organism that continued through the centuries while successive generations lived and died, that the thought of a divine purpose for the individual, a purpose transcending this present life, developed only when the breakdown of the nation as a political entity threw into prominence the individual and the question of personal destiny.

When a positive conviction arose of God's purpose holding each man and woman in being beyond the crisis of death, this conviction took the non-Platonic form of belief in the resurrection of the body. The religious difference between the Platonic belief in the immortality of the soul, and the Judaic-Christian belief in resurrection is that the latter postulates a special divine act of re-creation. This produces a sense of utter dependence upon God in the hour of death, a feeling that is in accordance with the biblical understanding of the human being as having been formed out of "the dust of the earth,"[7] a product (as we say today) of the slow evolution of life from its lowly beginnings in the primeval slime. Hence, in the Jewish and Christian conception, death is something real and fearful. It is not thought to be like walking from

[5]Gilbert Ryle's *The Concept of Mind* (London: Hutchinson & Co., Ltd., 1949, and New York: Barnes & Noble Books, 1975) is a classic statement of this critique.

[6]J. Pedersen, *Israel* (London: Oxford University Press, 1926), I, 170.

[7]Genesis 2:7; Psalm 103:14.

one room to another, or like taking off an old coat and putting on a new one. It means sheer unqualified extinction—passing out from the lighted circle of life into "death's dateless night." Only through the sovereign creative love of God can there be a new existence beyond the grave.

What does "the resurrection of the dead" mean? Saint Paul's discussion provides the basic Christian answer to this question.[8] His conception of the general resurrection (distinguished from the unique resurrection of Jesus) has nothing to do with the resuscitation of corpses in a cemetery. It concerns God's re-creation or reconstitution of the human psychophysical individual, not as the organism that has died but as a *soma pneumatikon*, a "spiritual body," inhabiting a spiritual world as the physical body inhabits our present material world.

A major problem confronting any such doctrine is that of providing criteria of personal identity to link the earthly life and the resurrection life. Paul does not specifically consider this question, but one may perhaps develop his thought along lines such as the following.[9]

Suppose, first, that someone—John Smith—living in the United States were suddenly and inexplicably to disappear before the eyes of his friends, and that at the same moment an exact replica of him were inexplicably to appear in India. The person who appears in India is exactly similar in both physical and mental characteristics to the person who disappeared in America. There is continuity of memory, complete similarity of bodily features including finger-prints, hair and eye coloration, and stomach contents, and also of beliefs, habits, emotions, and mental dispositions. Further, the "John Smith" replica thinks of himself as being the John Smith who disappeared in the United States. After all possible tests have been made and have proved positive, the factors leading his friends to accept "John Smith" as John Smith would surely prevail and would cause them to overlook even his mysterious transference from one continent to another, rather than treat "John Smith," with all of John Smith's memories and other characteristics, as someone other than John Smith.

Suppose, second, that our John Smith, instead of inexplicably disappearing, dies, but that at the moment of his death a "John Smith" replica, again complete with memories and all other characteristics, appears in India. Even with the corpse on our hands, we would, I think, still have to accept this "John Smith" as the John Smith who had died. We would just have to say that he had been miraculously re-created in another place.

Now suppose, third, that on John Smith's death the "John Smith" replica

---

[8] I Corinthians 15.

[9] The following paragraphs are adapted, with permission, from a section of my article, "Theology and Verification," published in *Theology Today* (April 1960) and reprinted in *The Existence of God* (New York: The Macmillan Company, 1964) and elsewhere. A fascinating recent argument for the personal identity of an original and his or her replica is offered by Derek Parfitt in *Reasons and Persons* (New York: Oxford University Press, 1985).

appears, not in India, but as a resurrection replica in a different world altogether, a resurrection world inhabited only by resurrected persons. This world occupies its own space distinct from that with which we are now familiar. That is to say, an object in the resurrection world is not situated at any distance or in any direction from the objects in our present world, although each object in either world is spatially related to every other object in the same world.

This supposition provides a model by which one may begin to conceive of the divine re-creation of the embodied human personality. In this model, the element of the strange and mysterious has been reduced to a minimum by following the view of some of the early Church Fathers that the resurrection body has the same shape as the physical body,[10] and ignoring Paul's own hint that it may be as unlike the physical body as a full grain of wheat differs from the wheat seed.[11]

What is the basis for this Judaic-Christian belief in the divine re-creation or reconstitution of the human personality after death? There is, of course, an argument from authority, in that life after death is taught throughout the New Testament (although very rarely in the Old Testament). More basically, though, belief in the resurrection arises as a corollary of faith in the sovereign purpose of God, which is not restricted by death and which holds us in being beyond our natural mortality. In a similar vein it is argued that if it be the divine plan to create finite persons to exist in fellowship with God, then it contradicts both that intention and God's love for the human creatures if God allows men and women to pass out of existence when the divine purpose for them still remains largely unfulfilled.

It is this promised fulfillment of God's purpose for the individual, in which the full possibilities of human nature will be realized, that constitutes the "heaven" symbolized in the New Testament as a joyous banquet in which all and sundry rejoice together. As we saw when discussing the problem of evil, it is questionable whether any theodicy can succeed without drawing into itself this eschatological[12] faith in an eternal, and therefore infinite, good which thus outweighs all the pains and sorrows that have been endured on the way to it.

Balancing the idea of heaven in Christian tradition is the idea of hell. This, too, is relevant to the problem of theodicy. Just as the reconciling of God's goodness and power with the fact of evil requires that out of the travail of history there shall come in the end an eternal good for humanity, so likewise it would seem to preclude eternal human misery. The only kind of evil that is finally incompatible with God's unlimited power and love would be utterly

[10]For example, Irenaeus, *Against Heresies*, Book II, Chap. 34, para. 1.

[11]I Corinthians 15:37.

[12]From the Greek *eschaton*, end.

pointless and wasted suffering, pain which is never redeemed and worked into the fulfilling of God's good purpose. Unending torment would constitute precisely such suffering; for being eternal, it could never lead to a good end beyond itself. Thus, hell as conceived by its enthusiasts, such as Augustine or Calvin, is a major part of the problem of evil! If hell is construed as eternal torment, the theological motive behind the idea is directly at variance with the urge to seek a theodicy. However, it is by no means clear that the doctrine of eternal punishment can claim a secure New Testament basis.[13] If, on the other hand, "hell" means a continuation of the purgatorial suffering often experienced in this life, and leading eventually to the high good of heaven, it no longer stands in conflict with the needs of theodicy. Again, the idea of hell may be deliteralized and valued as a powerful and pregnant symbol of the grave responsibility inherent in our human freedom in relation to our Maker.

## DOES PARAPSYCHOLOGY HELP?

The spiritualist movement claims that life after death has been proved by cases of communication between the living and the "dead." During the closing quarter of the nineteenth century and the decades of the present century this claim has been made the subject of careful and prolonged study by a number of responsible and competent persons.[14] This work, which may be approximately dated from the founding in London of the Society for Psychical Research in 1882, is known either by the name adopted by that society or, more commonly today, as parapsychology.

Approaching the subject from the standpoint of our interest in this chapter, we may initially divide the phenomena studied by the parapsychologist into two groups. There are those that involve no reference to the idea of a life after death, chief among these being psychokinesis (PK) and extrasensory perception (ESP) in its various forms (such as telepathy, clairvoyance, and precognition). There are also those phenomena that raise the question of personal survival after death, such as the apparitions and other sensory manifestations of dead persons and the "spirit messages" received through mediums. This division is, however, only of preliminary use, for ESP has emerged as a clue to the understanding of much that occurs in the second group. We shall begin

[13]The Greek word *aionios*, which is used in the New Testament and which is usually translated as "eternal" or "everlasting," can bear either this meaning or the more limited meaning of "for the aeon, or age."

[14]The list of past presidents of the Society for Psychical Research includes the philosophers Henri Bergson, William James, Hans Driesch, Henry Sidgwick, F. C. S. Schiller, C. D. Broad, and H. H. Price; the psychologists William McDougall, Gardner Murphy, Franklin Prince, and R. H. Thouless; the physicists Sir William Crookes, Sir Oliver Lodge, Sir William Barrett, and Lord Rayleigh; and the classicist Gilbert Murray.

with a brief outline of the reasons that have induced the majority of workers in this field to be willing to postulate so strange an occurrence as telepathy.

Telepathy is a name for the mysterious fact that sometimes a thought in the mind of one person apparently causes a similar or associated thought to occur to someone else when there are no normal means of communication between them, and under circumstances such that mere coincidence seems to be excluded.

For example, one person may draw a series of pictures or diagrams on paper and somehow transmit an impression of these to someone else in another room who then draws recognizable reproductions of them. This might well be a coincidence in the case of a single successful reproduction; but can a series consist entirely of coincidences?

Experiments have been devised to measure the probability of chance coincidence in supposed cases of telepathy. In the simplest of these, cards printed in turn with five different symbols are used. A pack of fifty, consisting of ten bearing each symbol, is then thoroughly shuffled, and the sender concentrates on the cards one at a time while the receiver (who of course can see neither sender nor cards) tries to write down the correct order of symbols. This procedure is repeated, with constant reshuffling, hundreds or thousands of times. Since there are only five different symbols, a random guess would stand one chance in five of being correct. Consequently, on the assumption that only "chance" is operating, the receiver should be right in about 20 percent of his or her tries and wrong in about 80 percent; the longer the series, the closer should be the approach to this proportion. However, good telepathic subjects are right in a larger number of cases than can be reconciled with random guessing. The deviation from chance expectation can be converted mathematically into "odds against chance" (increasing as the proportion of hits is maintained over a longer and longer series of tries). In this way, odds of over a million to one have been recorded. J. B. Rhine (Duke University) has reported results showing "antichance" values ranging from seven (which equals odds against chance of 100,000 to one) to eighty-two (which converts the odds against chance to billions).[15] The work of both these researchers has been criticized, and a complex controversy surrounds them; on the other hand, other researchers have recorded similar results.[16] In the light of these reports, it is difficult to deny that some positive factor, and not merely "chance," is operating. "Telepathy" is simply a name for this unknown positive factor.

[15]J. B. Rhine, *Extrasensory Perception* (Boston: Society for Psychical Research, 1935), Table XLIII, p. 162. See also Rhine, *New Frontiers of the Mind* (New York: Farrar and Rinehart, Inc., 1937), pp. 69f.

[16]The most comprehensive up-to-date account of the evidence for ESP, together with competent discussions of its significance, is to be found in Benjamin Wolman, ed., *Handbook of Parapsychology* (New York: Van Nostrand, 1977). For the important Russian work see L. L. Vasiliev, *Experiments in Distant Influence* (previously *Experiments in Mental Suggestion*, 1963) (New York: E. O. Dutton, 1976).

How does telepathy operate? Only negative conclusions seem to be justified to date. It can, for example, be said with reasonable certainty that telepathy does not consist of any kind of physical radiation analogous to radio waves. First, telepathy is not delayed or weakened in proportion to distance, as are all known forms of radiation; second, there is no organ in the brain or elsewhere that can plausibly be regarded as its sending or receiving center. Telepathy appears to be a purely mental occurrence.

It is not, however, a matter of transferring or transporting a thought out of one mind into another—if, indeed, such an idea makes sense at all. The telepathized thought does not leave the sender's consciousness in order to enter that of the receiver. What happens would be better described by saying that the sender's thought gives rise to a mental "echo" in the mind of the receiver. This "echo" occurs at the unconscious level, and consequently the version of it that rises into the receiver's consciousness may be only fragmentary and may be distorted or symbolized in various ways, as in dreams.

According to one theory that has been tentatively suggested to explain telepathy, our minds are separate and mutually insulated only at the conscious (and preconscious) level, but at the deepest level of the unconscious we are constantly influencing one another, and it is at this level that telepathy takes place.[17]

How is a telepathized thought directed to one particular receiver among so many? Apparently the thoughts are directed by some link of emotion or common interest. For example, two friends are sometimes telepathically aware of any grave crisis or shock experienced by the other, even though they are at opposite ends of the earth.

We shall turn now to the other branch of parapsychology, which has more obvious bearing upon our subject. The *Proceedings of the Society for Psychical Research* contain a large number of carefully recorded and apparently satisfactorily attested cases of the appearance of the figure of someone who has recently died to living people (in rare instances to more than one at a time) who were, in many cases, at a distance and unaware of the death. The S.P.R. reports also establish beyond reasonable doubt that the minds that operate in the mediumistic trance, purporting to be spirits of the departed, sometimes give personal information that the medium could not have acquired by normal means, and at times even give information, later verified, that had not been known to any living person.[18]

On the other hand, physical happenings such as the "materializations" of

---

[17]Whateley Carington, *Telepathy* (London: Methuen, 1945), Chaps. 6–8. See also H. L. Edge, R. L. Morris, J. H. Rushand, and J. Palmer, *Foundations of Parapsychology* (London: Routledge, 1986).

[18]A famous example is the Chaffin will case, recounted in many books, such as C. D. Broad, *Lectures on Psychical Research* (London: Routledge & Kegan Paul and New York: Humanities Press, 1962), pp. 137–39. (This, incidentally, remains one of the best books on parapsychology.)

spirit forms in a visible and tangible form, are much more doubtful. However, even if we discount the entire range of physical phenomena, it remains true that the best cases of trance utterance are impressive and puzzling, and taken at face value are indicative of survival and communication after death. If, through a medium, one talks with an intelligence that gives a coherent impression of being an intimately known friend who has died and who establishes identity by a wealth of private information and indefinable personal characteristics—as has occasionally happened—then we cannot dismiss without careful trial the theory that what is taking place is the return of a consciousness from the spirit world.

However, the advance of knowledge in the other branch of parapsychology, centering upon the study of extrasensory perception, has thrown unexpected light upon this apparent commerce with the departed, for it suggests that unconscious telepathic contact between the medium and his or her client is an important and possibly a sufficient explanatory factor. This was vividly illustrated by the experience of two women who decided to test the spirits by taking into their minds, over a period of weeks, the personality and atmosphere of an entirely imaginary character in an unpublished novel written by one of them. After thus filling their minds with the characteristics of this fictitious person, they went to a reputable medium, who proceeded to describe accurately their imaginary friend as a visitant from beyond the grave and to deliver appropriate messages from him.

An even more striking case is that of the "direct voice" medium (a medium in whose séances the voice of the communicating "spirit" is heard apparently speaking out of the air) who produced the spirit of one "Gordon Davis," who spoke in his own recognizable voice, displayed considerable knowledge about Gordon Davis, and remembered his death. This was extremely impressive until it was discovered that Gordon Davis was still alive; he was a real-estate agent and had been trying to sell a house at the time when the séance took place![19]

Such cases suggest that genuine mediums are simply persons of exceptional telepathic sensitiveness who unconsciously derive the "spirits" from their clients' minds.

In connection with "ghosts," in the sense of apparitions of the dead, it has been established that there can be "meaningful hallucinations," the source of which is almost certainly telepathic. To quote a classic and somewhat dramatic example: a woman sitting by a lake sees the figure of a man run toward the lake and throw himself in. A few days later a man commits suicide by throwing himself into this same lake. Presumably, the explanation of the

---

[19]S. G. Soal, "A Report of Some Communications Received through Mrs. Blanche Cooper," Sec. 4, *Proceedings of the Society for Psychical Research*, XXXV, 560–89.

vision is that the man's thought while he was contemplating suicide had been telepathically projected onto the scene via the woman's mind.[20]

In many of the cases recorded there is delayed action. The telepathically projected thought lingers in the recipient's unconscious mind until a suitable state of inattention to the outside world enables it to appear to the conscious mind in a dramatized form—for example, by a hallucinatory voice or vision—by means of the same mechanism that operates in dreams.

If phantoms of the living can be created by previously experienced thoughts and emotions of the person whom they represent, the parallel possibility arises that phantoms of the dead are caused by thoughts and emotions that were experienced by the person represented when he or she was alive. In other words, perhaps ghosts may be "psychic footprints," a kind of mental trace left behind by the dead but not involving the presence or even the continued existence of those whom they represent.

## RESUSCITATION CASES

Yet another range of phenomena that have recently attracted considerable interest consists of reports of the experiences of people who have been resuscitated after having been declared dead.[21] The periods during which they were apparently dead vary from a few seconds to twenty minutes or even more. These reports include the following elements, thought not usually all on the same occasion: an initial loud noise; a sensation as of being drawn through a dark tunnel-like space; emergence into a "world" of light and beauty; meeting with relatives and friends who had died; encounter with a "being of light" of immense moral or spiritual impressiveness, who is assumed by Christians to be Christ and by others to be an angel or a deity; an extremely vivid and almost instantaneous visual review of one's life; approach to a border, sensed to be the final division between this life and the next; and being sent or drawn back to the earthly body. Generally, those who have had this kind of experience are reluctant to speak about such hard-to-describe and hard-to-believe phenomena, but characteristically their attitude toward death has changed and they now think of their own future death without fear or even with positive anticipation.

[20]F. W. H. Myers, *Human Personality and Its Survival of Bodily Death* (London: Longmans, Green, & Co., 1903 and New York: Arno Press, 1975), I, 270–71. This is a classic work, still of great interest.

[21]The recent wave of interest began with the publication in 1975 of Raymond Moody's *Life after Life* (Atlanta: Mockingbird Books), and has been fed by a growing number of other books, including Raymond Moody, *Reflections on Life after Life* (New York: Bantam Books, 1977); Karlis Otis and Erlendur Haraldsson, *At the Hour of Death* (New York: Avon Books, 1977); Maurice Rawlings, *Beyond Death's Door* (Nashville: Thomas Nelson, Inc., 1978, and London: Sheldon Press, 1979).

Prior to such visual and auditory sequences there is also often an "out-of-the-body" experience, a consciousness of floating above one's own body and seeing it lying in bed or on the ground or the operating table. There is a growing literature concerning such "out-of-the-body" experiences, whether at the time of death or during life.[22]

Whether or not the resuscitation cases give us reports of the experiences of people who have actually died, and thus provide information about a life to come, it is at present impossible to determine. Do these accounts describe the first phase of another life, or perhaps a transitional stage before the connection between mind and body is finally broken; or do they describe only the last flickers of dream activity before the brain finally loses oxygen? It is to be hoped that further research may find a way to settle this question.

All these considerations suggest the need for caution in assessing the findings of parapsychology.[23] However, this caution should lead to further investigations, not to a closing of the issues. In the meantime one should be careful not to confuse absence of knowledge with knowledge of absence.

---

[22]For example, Sylvan Muldoon and Hereward Carrington, *The Phenomena of Astral Projection* (London: Rider, 1951); Robert Crookall, *The Study and Practice of Astral Projection* (London: Aquarian Press, 1961); Celia Green, *Out-of-the-Body Experiences* (London: Hamish Hamilton, 1968); *Journeys Out of the Body* (New York: Doubleday & Co., Inc., 1971, and London: Souvenir Press, 1972); Benjamin Walker, *Beyond the Body* (London: Routledge & Kegan Paul, 1974).

[23]Philosophical discussions of parapsychology can be found in: C. D. Broad, *Religion, Philosophy and Psychical Research* (London: Routledge & Kegan Paul, 1953); James Wheatley and Hoyt Edge, eds., *Philosophical Dimensions of Parapsychology* (Springfield, Ill.; C Thomas, 1976); Shivesh Thakur, ed., *Philosophy and Psychical Research* (New York: Humanities Press, 1976); Jan Ludwig, ed., *Philosophy and Parapsychology* (Prometheus, 1978); Stephen Braude, *ESP and Psychokinesis: A Philosophical Examination* (Philadelphia: Temple University Press, 1980).

# CHAPTER 11

# Human Destiny: Karma and Reincarnation

## THE POPULAR CONCEPT

To nearly everyone formed by our western Atlantic culture it seems self-evident that we came into existence at conception or birth and shall see the last of this world at death: in other words, we are born only once and we die only once. However, to one brought up within a Hindu or Buddhist culture it seems self-evident that we have, on the contrary, lived many times before and must live many times again in this world. Each idea or theory involves its own difficulties, and I shall be pointing out presently some of the difficulties in the idea of reincarnation. But first let us take note of the main difficulty that Hindus, Buddhists, and others see in the western assumption. They point to the immense inequalities of human birth. One person is born with a healthy body and a high IQ, to loving parents with a good income in an advanced and affluent society, so that all the riches of human culture are available and the individual has considerable freedom to choose his or her own mode of life. Another is born with a crippled body and a low IQ, to unloving, unaffluent, and uncultured parents in a society in which that person is highly likely to become a criminal and to die an early and violent death. Is it fair that they should be born with such unequal opportunities? If a new soul is created whenever a new baby is conceived, can the Creator who is responsible for each soul's unequal endowment be described as loving? We have all heard the story of John Bradford, who saw a criminal being taken to be hung and said, "But for the grace of God there goes John Bradford." The story is edifying insofar as it reminds us of God's grace to John Bradford; but what about God's grace, or lack of it, to the condemned criminal? The more one contemplates the gross inequalities of human birth, and our western religious assumption that human beings are divinely created in these different conditions, the more one is likely to see grave injustices here.

The alternative assumption of the religions of Indian origin is that we have all lived before and that the conditions of our present life are a direct consequence of our previous lives. There is no arbitrariness, no randomness, no injustice in the inequalities of our human lot, but only cause and effect, the reaping now of what we have ourselves sown in the past. Our essential self continues from life to life, being repeatedly reborn or reincarnated, the state of its karma determining the circumstances of its next life.

In its more popular form in both East and West the doctrine of reincarnation holds that the conscious character-bearing and (in principle) memory-bearing self transmigrates from body to body. As we read in the *Bhagavad Gita*, "Just as a person casts off worn-out garments and puts on others that are new, even so does the embodied soul cast off worn-out bodies and takes on others that are new" (2, 13). On this conception it is possible to say that I—the "I" who am now conscious and who am now writing these words—have lived before and will live again, in other bodies. It must accordingly be in principle possible for me, in my present body, to remember my past lives, even though in fact the traumas of death and birth generally erase these memories, repressing them to a deep and normally inaccessible level of the unconscious. Occasionally, however, ordinary people do for some reason seem to remember fragments of a recent life; and these claimed memories of former lives are important, not only as evidence offered for rebirth, but also conceptually, as fixing what is meant by the doctrine. One may or may not find cases of this kind to be impressive, if they are offered as hard evidence for rebirth.[1] Nevertheless, the fact that supposed recollections of former lives are pointed to as evidence does mark out a particular content for the idea of rebirth. Let me, therefore, formulate a reincarnation hypothesis on the basis of these instances of claimed memories of former lives.

Consider the relation between the John Hick who is now writing, whom I shall call J. H.[66], and John Hick at the age of two, whom I shall call J. H.[2]. The main differences between them are, first, that J. H.[66] and J. H.[2] do not look at all like each other and, second, that their conscious selves are quite different. As to the first difference, no one shown a photo of J. H.[2] would know, without being told, that it is a photo of J. H[66] as he was sixty-four years ago, rather than that of almost anybody else at the age of two; for there is very little similarity

---

[1]There is an extensive literature reporting and discussing such cases. The most scientifically valuable are those of Professor Ian Stevenson: *Twenty Cases Suggestive of Reincarnation*, 2nd ed. (Charlottesville: University of Virginia Press, 1974); *Cases of the Reincarnation Type*, Vol. I: *Ten Cases in India*, Vol. II: *Ten Cases in Sri Lanka*, and Vol. III: *Twelve Cases in Lebanon and Turkey* (Charlottesville: University of Virginia Press, 1975–79).

of appearance between these two visible objects. As to the second difference, if one were to hear a recording of the two-year-old J. H. revealing his thoughts in words and other noises one would, I think, feel that J. H.[66] has a very different mind. No doubt the same basic personality traits are present in both the child and the man, but nevertheless the conscious self of the one is very different from the conscious self of the other—so much so that a comparison of the two would never by itself lead us to conclude that they are the same self. There are, then, immense differences between J. H.[2] and J. H.[66] from the points of view both of physical and of psychological description. Notwithstanding that, J. H.[66] does have at least one fragmentary memory of an event that was experienced by J. H.[2]. He remembers being told when his sister, who is two years younger than himself, was born. Thus there is a tenuous memory link connecting J. H.[66] with J. H.[2] despite all the dissimilarities that we have noted between them; and this fact reminds us that it is possible to speak of memory across the gap of almost any degree of physical and psychological difference.

Now let us see if we can say the same of someone who remembers a previous life. To spell this out in the well-known case of Shanti Devi: Lugdi—who was born in 1902, lived in Muthra, and died in 1924 as Mrs. Chaubey—was (presumably) very different as regards both physical and psychological descriptions from Shanti Devi, who was born in 1926 and lived at Delhi. But Shanti Devi claimed to have certain memories of people and events experienced by Lugdi, which are said to have been confirmed by impartial investigators. Our reincarnation hypothesis is that despite the differences between them, they are in fact the same person or self, in a sense comparable with that in which J. H.[66] is the same person as J. H.[2]. In speaking in this way of the same person being born in 1902 in one part of India, later dying, and then being born again in 1926 in another part of India, we are presupposing the existence of a continuing mental entity which I am calling the self or the person. The hypothesis we are considering is that just as J. H.[66] is the same person as J. H.[2], though at a later point in the history of that person, so also Shanti Devi is the same person as Lugdi, though at a later point in that person's history. The big difference—concerning which we have to ask whether it is *too* big a difference—is that now these are not earlier and later points in the same life but in two successive lives. They are, as it were, points in different volumes of the same multivolume work instead of in different chapters of the same volume.

Let us, then, consider the claim that all human selves have lived many times before, even though the great majority, even perhaps some 99 percent, have no memory of any such previous lives. The question I want to raise concerns the criteria by which someone living today is said to be the same person or self as someone who lived, say, 500 years ago of whom one has no knowledge or memory. For when we remove the connecting thread of memory, as we are doing in our present rebirth hypothesis, we have taken away one, and a very important one, of the three strands of continuity that constitute what we normally mean by the identity of a human individual through time. A second strand is bodily continuity, an unbroken existence through space and time from the newly born baby to the old person, a continuity stretching thus from the cradle to the grave. It may be that none of the atoms that composed the baby's body are now part of the adult's body. Nonetheless a continuously changing physical organism has existed and has been in principle observable, composed from moment to moment of slightly different populations of atoms, but with sufficient overlap of population and of configuration of population from moment to moment for it to constitute the same organism. However, this strand of bodily continuity is also taken away by our rebirth hypothesis, for there is no physical connection between someone living in the United States today and someone who lived, say, in China five hundred years ago. Nor does it even seem to be claimed by the doctrine of rebirth that there is any bodily resemblance; for it is said that one is sometimes born as a man, sometimes as a woman, sometimes in one and sometimes in another branch of the human race, and sometimes indeed (according to one version of the doctrine) as an animal or perhaps as an insect.

Thus, all that is left to be the bearer of personal identity is the third strand, which is the psychological continuity of a pattern of mental dispositions. It is this that now has to carry all the weight of the identity of two persons, one of whom is said to be a reincarnation of the other. For the only connection left, when memory and bodily continuity are excluded, lies in the psychological dispositions that constitute one's personal character. It is claimed that B, who is A reincarnated, has the same personality traits as A. If A was proud and intolerant, B will be proud and intolerant. If A becomes in the course of her life a great artist, B will start life with a strong artistic propensity. If A was kind and thoughtful, B will be kind and thoughtful. But much now depends, for the viability of the theory, upon the *degree* of similarity that is claimed to exist between the total personalities of A at $t^1$ and B at $t^2$. Many people are kind and thoughtful, or have artistic temperaments, or are proud and intolerant, but as long as they are distinct bodily beings with different and distinct streams of consciousness and memory, the fact that two individuals exhibit a common character trait, or even a number of such traits, does not lead us to identify them as the same person. In the case of people living at the same time, to do so would be a direct violation of the concept of "same person." In the case of people who are not alive at the same time such an identification is not ruled out with the same *a priori* logical definitiveness; but it is nevertheless beset with the most formidable difficulties. For the similarity between A ($t^1$) and B ($t^2$) must, in most cases, be so general as to be capable of numerous different exemplifications, since A and B may be of different races and sexes, and products of different civilizations, climates, and historical epochs. There can be *general* similarities of character, found in such qualities as selfishness and unselfishness, introverted or extroverted types of personality, artistic or practical bents, and in level of intelligence, between, let us say, a male Tibetan peasant of the twelfth century B.C.E. and a female American college graduate of the twentieth century C.E. However, such general similarities would never by themselves lead or entitle us to identify the two as the same person. Indeed, to make an identity claim on these grounds—in a case in which there is neither bodily continuity nor any link of memory—would commit us to the principle that all individuals who are not alive at the same time and who exhibit rather similar personality patterns are to be regarded as the same person. But in that case there would be far too many people who qualify under this criterion as being the same person. How many people of Lugdi's generation were as much like Shanti Devi in general character as Lugdi was? Probably many hundreds of thousands. How many people in the last generation before I was born had character traits similar to those that I have? Probably many hundreds of thousands. On this basis alone, then, it would never have occurred to anyone that Lugdi and Shanti Devi were the same person, or that I am the same person as any one particular individual who lived in the past. On this basis I could equally well be a reincarnation of any one of many thousands of people in each past generation. Thus, this criterion of character similarity is far too broad and permissive; if it establishes anything, it establishes much too much and becomes self-defeating.

Thus the idea of reincarnation in the sense of the transmigration of the self without memory of its previous lives from death in one body to birth in another is beset by conceptual difficulties.


## THE VEDĀNTIC CONCEPTION

Let us then turn to the more complex and subtle conception of reincarnation taught in Hindu Vedāntic philosophy. This is, of course, by no means the only school of Indian religious thought, but the Vedāntic conception of karma and rebirth is a central one from which most of the other schools differ only marginally. According to Advaita Vedānta, the ultimate reality—Brahman— is pure undifferentiated consciousness, beyond all qualities, including personality. The creative power of Brahman expresses itself in the existence of the universe, whose nature is *māyā*, which connotes unreality in the sense of being dependent and temporary. The infinite eternal consciousness becomes associated with *māyā* to constitute a plurality of temporary finite consciousnesess, *jīvātmans* or *jīvas*, which I shall call souls. These finite consciousnesses are products of *māyā*, and their very existence is a kind of illusion, the illusion namely of separateness from the one universal consciousness. In an often-used Vedāntic simile, Brahman is like Space and the individual souls are like space in jars. When the jars are destroyed, the space that they enclosed remains part of Space. Likewise, the souls merge into the infinite Brahman when the ignorance that constitutes their finite boundaries is removed in enlightenment.

There are, then, a limitless number of individual souls; and yet this plurality and individuality is ultimately illusory, for when different souls attain to consciousness of themselves as Brahman, the distinction between them ceases to exist: all souls as Brahman are one and the same. The theory of karma and rebirth is concerned with the soul and its evolution from the state of illusion to true self-consciousness. For the innumerable souls, as "sparks of divinity" that have become illusorily separated from their source, ground, and identity in Brahman, are being gradually purged of this illusion through a succession of rebirths, in a process that is eventually to culminate in the attainment of liberation and the realization of identity with the sole ultimate Reality, Brahman, unspoiled by any illusory sense of separate identity. (This conception has, of course, its affinities in the West in Neoplatonism and Gnosticism and in the recent theology of Paul Tillich).

There are, then, an infinity of souls existing beginninglessly throughout past time. But I, the conscious self now writing, and you, the conscious self now reading, are not—or rather are not consciously—any of these eternal souls. We are psychophysical egos, illusorily distinct persons of the kind that exist only in this realm of *māyā*. Whereas the psychophysical ego is a man or a woman, the soul is neither male nor female but includes (in Jung's terminology) the *animus* and *anima* aspects that, when embodied in varying proportions, constitute human masculinity and femininity. Whereas the psychophysical ego is not normally conscious of the eternal past of the soul, there are depths of the soul in which all this past experience is recorded. Each psychophysical ego is thus a temporary expression, or organ, or instrument of an eternal soul, one indeed of the succession of such expressions which constitute the successive rebirths of that soul. That the soul is involved in *māyā* means that it has become enclosed in a set of "bodies" or coverings, thought of on the analogy of a number of sheaths successively enclosing the blade of a sword, and all having to be discarded before the blade is free. There are three principal such "bodies" or sheaths: the gross body (*sthūla śarīra*), the subtle body (*sūksma śarīra* or *liṅga śarīra*), and the causal body (*kāraṇa śarīra*). So far as the essential logic of the idea of rebirth is concerned, we can combine the latter two into one, the "subtle body," and concentrate upon the relation between this and the "gross body." The "gross body" is the physical organism that begins to be formed at conception and begins to disintegrate at death. It is survived by the "subtle body," which then influences the development of another physical body as its next vehicle of incarnation. It must, however, at once be added that the phrase "subtle body" is likely to be seriously misleading to the western mind, for the "subtle body" is not, in the philosophically sophisticated versions of the theory, conceived of as a material entity in the western sense of "material." It does not occupy space, has no shape or size, and is indeed not a body at all in our western sense of the term. It is, however, material in the quite different sense given by the fundamental Indian dichotomy between consciousness and everything that lacks consciousness and is called *prakrti*—"nature" or "matter"—this being identical with *māyā*. In western terms the subtle body must accordingly be described as a mental rather than as a physical entity; indeed, one Hindu expositor speaks of it simply as "the psychical part of the psychophysical organism."[2] So far as its function in the theory of rebirth is concerned, we may describe the *liṅga śarīra* as a mental entity or substance that is modified by, or registers and thus (metaphorically) "embodies," the moral, aesthetic, intellectual, and spiritual dispositions that have been built up in the course of living a human life, or rather in living a succession of human, and perhaps also nonhuman, lives. These modifications of the subtle body are called *saṁskāras*, impressions. But they are not thought of on the analogy of static impressions, like marks on paper, but rather as dynamic impressions, modifications of a living organism expressed in its pattern of behavior. We ordinarily think of the human mind and personality as being modified in all sorts of ways by its own volitions and its responses to its experience. A repeated indulgence in selfish policies reinforces one's egoistic tendencies; a constant exercise of the discipline of precise thought makes for more lucid and exact thinking; devoted attention to one or another of the arts quickens and deepens one's aesthetic sensibilities; spiritual meditation opens the self to the influence of a larger environment; and so on. These familiar facts can be expressed by saying that the *liṅga śarīra* is the seat of the various emotional, spiritual, moral, aesthetic, and intellectual modifications that are happening to us all the time in the course of our human existence. Such modifications are most adequately characterized in contemporary western categories as mental dispositions.

We have already noted that the subtle body belongs to the material (*prakrti*) side of the fundamental dichotomy between consciousness and *prakrti*; and it is for this reason that it is appropriate in the context of Indian thought to call it a body. For being finite, changeable, and devoid of consciousness, it has far more in common with the physical body than with the soul. To appreciate this we have to conceive of thoughts, emotions, and desires as things, and as things capable of existing apart from consciousness, as dispositional energies that, when linked with consciousness, can guide action. Through like grouping with like in mutual reinforcement, such dispositions form relatively stable and enduring structures whose "shape" is the character of the person whose thoughts have formed it. Such a dispositional structure survives the extinction of consciousness in death and continues to exist as an entity, the subtle body or *liṅga śarīra*, which will later become linked to a new conscious organism. It

[2]Suryanarayana Sastri, "The Doctrine of Reincarnation in Educational Work," *Indian Philosophical Annual*, 1965, p. 165. Generally, on Hindu and Buddhist conceptions of reincarnation, see Wendy Doniger O'Flaherty, ed., *Karma and Rebirth in Classical Indian Traditions* (Berkeley: University of California Press, 1980).

is thus very close to what C. D. Broad has called the "psychic factor."[3] Broad developed his concept of the psychic factor to provide a possible explanation of the phenomenon of trance mediumship. When an individual dies, the mental aspect persists, not however as a complete conscious personality, but as a constellation of mental elements—dispositions, memories, desires, fears, etc.—constituting a psychic factor, which may hold together for a considerable time or may quickly disintegrate into scattered fragments. Broad suggested that such a psychic grouping, sufficiently cohesive to be identified as consisting of the memories and dispositional characteristics of a particular deceased individual, may become connected with a medium in a state of trance, thus generating a temporary conscious personality which is a conflation of certain persisting mental elements of the deceased together with the living structure of the medium. The theory of reincarnation can be seen as taking this concept further—as indeed Broad himself noted[4]—and claiming that the psychic factor that separates itself from the body at death subsequently becomes fused, not with the developed life structure of a medium, but with the still undeveloped life structure of a human embryo. It then influences the growth of the embryo, as a factor additional to its physical genetic inheritance.

If we ask why Hindus believe that this is a true account of the facts of human existence, there are three interlocking answers. One is that it is a revealed truth taught in the Vedas. A second is that reincarnation is a hypothesis that makes sense of many aspects of human life, including the inequalities of human birth; I shall return to this presently. The third is that there are the fragmentary memories of former lives to which we have already referred and also, even more important, the much fuller memories that are attained by those who have achieved *moksa*, liberation and enlightenment. It is claimed that the yogi, on attaining *moksa*, remembers all his or her former existences, seeing the karmic connection that runs through a succession of apparently different and unrelated lives. This last item is for many in India the most important of all grounds for belief in reincarnation.

Now, what exactly does reincarnation mean when it is thus given factual anchorage by a claimed retrospective yogic memory of a series of lives that were not linked by memory while they were being lived? The picture before us is of, say, a hundred distinct empirical selves living their different lives one after another and being as distinct from each other as any other set of a hundred lives; and yet differing from a random series of a hundred lives in that the last member of the series attains a level of consciousness at which he or she is aware of the entire series. Further, she remembers the entire series as lives which she, now in this higher state of awareness, has herself lived. Yet there is something logically odd about such "remembering," which prompts

---

[3]C. D. Broad, *The Mind and Its Place in Nature* (London: Routledge & Kegan Paul Ltd., 1925, and New York: Humanities Press, 1976), pp. 536ff.

[4]*Ibid.*, p. 551.

one to put it in quotation marks. For this higher state of consciousness did not experience those earlier lives and therefore it cannot in any ordinary sense be said to remember them. Rather, it is in a state *as though* it had experienced them, although in fact it did not.

The claim here, then, is that there will in the future exist a supernormal state of consciousness, in which "memories" of a long succession of different lives occur. However, this leaves open the question of how best to describe such a state of affairs. Let us name the first person in the series A and the last Z. Are we to say that B–Z are a series of reincarnations of A? If we do, we shall be implicitly stipulating the following definition: given two or more non-contemporaneous human lives, if there is a higher consciousness in which they are all "remembered," then each later individual in the series is defined as being a reincarnation of each earlier individual. But reincarnation so defined is a concept far removed from the idea that if I am A, then *I* shall be repeatedly reborn as B–Z. Further, there is no conceptual reason why we should even stipulate that the different lives must be noncontemporaneous. If it is possible for a higher consciousness to "remember" any number of different lives, there seems in principle to be no reason why it should not "remember" lives that have been going on at the same time as easily as lives that have been going on at different times. Indeed, we can conceive of an unlimited higher consciousness in which "memories" occur of all human lives that have ever been lived. Then *all* human lives, however different from their own several points of view, would be connected via a higher consciousness in the way postulated by the idea of reincarnation. It would then be proper to say of *any* two lives, whether earlier and later or contemporaneous, that the one individual is a different incarnation of the other. Thus it seems that there are conceptual difficulties in the idea of reincarnation in its more subtle Vedāntic form as well as in its more popular form.

Let us now return to the inequalities of human birth and ask whether the idea of reincarnation can after all really help to explain these. Either there is a first life, characterized by initial human differences, or else (as in the Vedāntic philosophy) there is no first life but a beginningless regress of incarnations. In the latter case the explanation of the inequalities of our present life is endlessly postponed and never achieved, for we are no nearer to an ultimate explanation of the circumstances of our present birth when we are told that they are consequences of a previous life, if that previous life has in turn to be explained by reference to a yet previous life, and that by reference to another, and so on in an infinite regress. One can affirm the beginningless character of the soul's existence in this way, but one cannot then claim that it renders either intelligible or morally acceptable the inequalities found in our present human lot. The solution has not been produced but only postponed to infinity. If instead we were to postulate a first life (as Hinduism does not), we should then have to hold either that souls are created as identical psychic atoms or else as embodying, at least in germ, the differences that have subsequently developed. If the latter, the problem of human inequality arises in full force at the point of that initial creation; if the former, it arises as forcefully with regard to the environment that has produced all the manifold differences that have subsequently arisen between initially identical units. Thus if there is a divine Creator, it would seem that that Creator cannot escape along any of these paths from an ultimate responsibility for the character of the creation, including the gross inequalities inherent within it.

## A DEMYTHOLOGIZED INTERPRETATION

The possibility of construing reincarnation as an unverifiable and unfalsifiable metaphysical idea takes us to the borders of a third form of the doctrine. In this form it is a mythological expression of the fact that all our actions have effects upon some part of the human community and have to be borne, for good or ill, by others in the future. This ethical sense has been attributed by some scholars to the Buddha, notably by J. G. Jennings.[5] He says, "Disbelieving in the permanence of the individual soul he [the Buddha] could not accept the Hindu doctrine of Karma implying the transmigration of the soul at death to a new body; but believing fully in moral responsibility and the consequences of all acts, words, and thoughts, he fully accepted the doctrine of Karma in another sense, implying the transmission of the effects of actions from one generation of men to all succeeding generations" (p. xlvii). Again, Jennings says, "Assuming the common origin and the fundamental unity of all life and spirit, he [the Buddha] assumed the unity of the force of Karma upon the living material of the whole world, and the doctrine of Karma taught by him is collective and not individual" (p. xxv).

On this view karma, with reincarnation as its mythological expression, is really a moral truth, a teaching of universal human responsibility. All our deeds affect the human future, as the life of each of us has in its turn been affected by those who have lived before us. Instead of individual threads of karmic history there is the universal network of the karma of humanity, to which each contributes and by which each is affected. Understood in this manner, the idea of reincarnation is a way of affirming the corporate unity of the human race, and the responsibility of each toward the whole of which he or she is a part. We are not monadic individuals, but mutually interacting parts of the one human world in which the thoughts and acts of each reverberate continually for good or ill through the lives of others. As the ways in which men and women have lived in the past have formed the world in which we now have to live, so we in turn are now forming the world in which future generations will have to dwell. As our inherited world, or state of world karma, has formed us as individuals born into it, so we in turn are helping to

[5]J. G. Jennings, *The Vedāntic Buddhism of the Buddha* (London: Oxford University Press, 1948).

shape the environment that is to form those who live after us. So conceived, the idea of karma has immense practical implications at a time when the nations are grappling with the threat of the pollution of our human environment, with problems of environmental planning and conservation, with the prevention of nuclear war, with the control of the population explosion, with racial conflict, and with so many other problems concerned with the ways in which the actions of each individual and group affect the welfare of all. Seen in this way, karma is an ethical doctrine. And both the more popular idea of the transmigration of souls and the more philosophical idea of the continuity of a "subtle body" from individual to individual in succeeding generations can be seen as mythological expressions of this great moral truth.

Most western philosophers would probably have no difficulty accepting this last form of reincarnation doctrine, for it is a vivid affirmation of human unity; the world today is such that if we do not unite in a common life, we are only too likely to find ourselves united in a common death. But to what extent this is an acceptable interpretation of the idea of rebirth, which has for some thousands of years been cherished by the great religions of India, is not for us to say.

# For Further Reading

## On the Nature of Religion:

WILFRED CANTWELL SMITH, *The Meaning and End of Religion*, 1962, new ed. New York: Harper & Row, and London: Sheldon Press, 1978.

## On the Theistic Arguments:

RICHARD SWINBURNE, *The Existence of God*. New York: Oxford University Press, 1979.

## On the Idea of Revelation:

H. RICHARD NIEBUHR, *The Meaning of Revelation*. New York: Macmillan Publishing Co., Inc., 1941.

## On the Problem of Evil:

JOHN HICK, *Evil and the God of Love*, 2nd ed. London: Macmillan & Company, Ltd., and New York: Harper & Row, 1978. (Reissued, Macmillan, 1987.)

EDWARD MADDEN AND PETER HARE, *Evil and the Concept of God*. Springfield, Ill.: Charles C Thomas, 1968.

## On Death and Immortality:

JOHN HICK, *Death and Eternal Life*. London: Collins, and New York: Harper & Row, 1976. (Reissued, Macmillan, 1987.)

PAUL AND LINDA BADHAM, *Immortality or Extinction?* London: Macmillan & Company, Ltd., and New York: Barnes & Noble, 1981.

## On the Relation Between Religions:

WILFRED CANTWELL SMITH, *Towards a World Theology*. London: Macmillan & Company, Ltd., and Philadelphia: Westminster Press, 1981.

JOHN HICK, *An Interpretation of Religion*. New Haven: Yale University Press, and London: Macmillan, 1989.

# Index